E-Resources and Digital Services

E-RESOURCES AND DIGITAL SERVICES

Dr. V K J Jeevan

Ess Ess Publications

4837/24, Ansari Road, Darya Ganj,
New Delhi-110002
✆ : 23260807, 41563444
Fax : 011-41563334
E-mail: info@essessreference.com
url:http://www.essessreference.com

First Edition 2011

Published by SUMIT SETHI
for **Ess Ess Publications**
4837/24, Ansari Road, Darya Ganj,
New Delhi - 110 002
Ph. : 23260807, 41563444
Fax : 011-41563334
E-mail: info@essessreference.com
url:http://www.essessreference.com

ISBN : 978-81-7000-652-7

Price : Rs. 700/-

Laser Typesetting:
Mukesh Graphics
T-1264, Mangolpuri, New Delhi
Ph. : 9899079035, 27918550
E-mail:mukeshgraphics29@gmail.com

Printed at :
Print Line

to undying memories of
MY MOTHER

CONTENTS

Contents

PREFACE

The intrusion of technology and electronic resources into the portals of library has made challenges and more challenges for library professionals of today. Coupled with this is the emancipation of users from the four walls of library making them more demanding and less satisfied with our age old tools and techniques. User wants the easiness with which they search and access an internet resource with library content also, irrespective of the form and format in which it is locally available. There are also various specialists encroaching into our professional territory, be it the computer specialist, the information officer, public relations officer, intellectual property expert, research analyst. Day by day the demands on libraries and librarians are on the rise, though they are being challenged on various aspects such as the operational freedom, procedural wrangles, non-library expert committees, funds, infrastructure, technology etc. No doubt library has a future only if librarians convert these challenges as assets in enriching the information experience of users.

This book is an outcome of the interactions a practicing librarian has on different occasions with few such challenges. The book is organised in 12 chapters. The first chapter on e-resources presents a step by step account of how effectively a library should take advantage of such dynamic, functional and nascent resources. The second chapter surveys the response towards open access by few prominent scholarly publishers providing a non-publisher institutional dissemination of scholarly publications. Distance education is emerging as a major teaching learning outlet in many developing countries. How digital media can play a lead role in distance education is highlighted in chapter 3. DELNET emerges no doubt as the best performing city network of libraries in the country and its services especially in the areas of document delivery and inter library loan are very noteworthy. The next chapter provides a thought on how these key services could come to the rescue of geographically disperse wide and varied category of resource starved distance learners. Chapter 5 presents a case study on the crucial problem of price verification of books purchased in a library. The next chapter is on research collaboration of different categories of library professionals; teachers, librarians and library science students. The next two chapters deal with public libraries. How public libraries can be used effectively for spreading science awareness is discussed in chapter 7. Chapter 8 throws light on the need of digital enabling of public libraries for empowering the citizens. The seminal thoughts of Dr. S R Ranganathan finds interesting applications in different emerging areas of library science and chapter 9 suggests possible applications of his research on digital libraries. Prof. P N Kaula lived a life rich in legacy and professionalism and no doubt his heroisms continue to inspire professionals for many years to come; Chapter 10 is a reflection of this aspect. Chapter 11 suggests libraries should practice stock accountability than stock verification as it is the duty of a library to maintain all resources on its stacks what is reflected in the catalogue. The last chapter is about some of the anomalies with respect to library positions in the aftermath of the adoption of the sixth pay commission regulations.

Thanks are due to the authors whose papers I have referred and they showed the right path for me to pursue. Peers, teachers, friends, professional colleagues and juniors provided ample encouragement in my academic pursuits. My primary gratitude goes to my previous employer, Indian Institute of Technology, Kharagpur and present employer, Indira Gandhi National Open University, New Delhi for the high academic ideals, excellent infrastructure and the good company of educated community they provide. With a series of health problems, my mother, the most selfless person I ever met so far in this life, left this earth before the publication of this book. I am going to miss that sparkle in her eyes whenever I show my new publication. I can remember only with tears how she lost her sleep every night to wake me up for my early morning studies when I was a student. My father, brothers and families, and in-laws deserve special mention for their concern. This book has become a reality due to the encouragement and support of my wife and children. I have great respect for the readers and earnestly wait for their valuable comments. Mr. Sumit Sethi and his team at Ess Ess Publications deserve special approbation for bringing out this publication in a pleasing manner in short time.

Delhi **(Dr. V K J Jeevan)**
April 2011

Books by the same author from Ess Ess Publications

1. **Digital Libraries, ISBN: 81-7000-376-8, 2004, 415 pages, Price: Rs.900**

The book is organized into 6 parts and 26 chapters. The first part' digital libraries' deals with three different aspects of the emerging area such digitizing scholarly journals, infrastructure to be created for and the problems to be tackled while proceeding with digital library development and the best practices to be followed by libraries before venturing into digitization projects. 8 chapters in the second part concentrate on the virtues of using computers and information technology for better information organization and rendering attractive user focused information services. The third part of the book in four chapters descries the information management and its facets in specific disciplines of technology, science, engineering, and management. Part 4 of the book discusses issues like the content creation role of library professionals, constraints concerning representation of time and version control specifically with respect to electronic information. The three chapters in part 5 deal with problems and prospects of a shared library access oriented approach as a result of increasing dependence on costly international publications for higher education and research. Part 6 of the book, in 6 chapters expresses the growing concern of an alert information professional on the present state of affairs in a 'free for all anti-student quantity centred quality devoid' library and information science education. This book shall serve as an immensely helpful tool for professionals and students who want to know more about 'Digital Libraries'.

2. **Computer @ Libraries, ISBN: 81-7000-445-4, 2006, xxi, 506 pages, Price: Rs.1075**

This book is organized in 6 parts 25 chapters. The first part state of the art' talks about the relevance of Ranganathan in the digital era, the trends of job opportunities in the library profession, quality auditing of our libraries on the lines of the nationwide procedure adopted in US, managing knowledge and information management, the possibilities and dangers in managing knowledge, e-learning library science, and preserving the intellectual output of developing countries with an illustration of superconductivity literature. The second part of the book covers two aspects of book acquisition, from just buying books to collection development and electronically enabling book collection and their access, the futility of hanging to unilateral regime like the present GOC which totally bypasses the diverse membership it accommodated once. Part three throws light on IT enabling public libraries, information support for rural development and National Library. Libraries and librarians have to deal with electronic contents in wide variety and more quantity these days and that is the subject matter of Part four. Part five encompasses different facets of computer applications in libraries. Part six is about the 'big bang' In Library science, digital libraries. It discusses how to build digital libraries in a pragmatic way, the most important ingredient for digital libraries, content, which are aplenty in developing countries. Archiving digital contents is the next step in maintaining digital libraries which also finds reference then the book discusses the difficulties libraries and librarians have to overcome before jumping into the bandwagon.

3. Library Personalization, ISBN 81-7000-500-0, 2007, xxxiv, 230 pages, Price: Rs. 600

Library Personalization provides the library with a viable mechanism to manipulate the information base using available technologies so that the library appears as a set of separate smaller libraries holding more effective content to individual users. It helps users to start with a generic library and by making selections and choices create a personal library with pre-selected and most relevant information resources. Also, the user can view the different services offered by the library through a single interface with links to different services and resources in multiple servers inside and outside the library. It has also been designed to enable faculty members and researchers, busy with teaching and research work, to save the considerable time spent in collecting information rather than using it. With the advent of electronic full text resources and especially the internet, users need a 'Web' like search and access at the click of a link facility for information resources stored in the library through personalization services. In the absence of such personal information support, users would be left to fend for themselves and forced to scan the information overload through library OPACs, electronic databases, networked electronic content etc., which may often lead to information under-use severely hampering research and teaching output. The book in 8 chapters with supporting details of implementation presents an interesting case study of personalization of library services from the Indian perspective.

1

E-RESOURCES

1. INTRODUCTION

Advances in information technology, urge for information providers to repackage and generate alternate products, demand of users to have easy to search, browse, retrieve and reuse mode of feature rich non print information sources all lead to the present trend of hybrid libraries. In such libraries irrespective of the form and format, content is acquired, processed and serviced. It is difficult to think of even public libraries without some content in electronic format, be it the free CD-ROMs that accompany magazines or books. In the case of higher education and research libraries, the dependence on e-resources is increasing rapidly over the last few years.

2. TYPES OF E-RESOURCES

Any information source available in electronic format which can be used to meet the information requirements of users is termed as e-resource. There are many types of e-resources, but the three major categories which are of importance in the context of higher education and research libraries are:

e-journals or electronic journals which are electronic equivalents of print journals/serials

e-books or electronic books which are nothing but monographs available for electronic access like e-journals but in many cases backed by a digital rights management system.

e-databases which are full text, bibliographic, numeric etc., databases holding a wide variety of information in one product/platform

Libraries do have variations of these products before the advent of web but the web access of these resources further improved the functionality of each of these products in a variety of ways to make it more appealing to the information clientele of today.

3. ACQUIRING E-RESOURCES

There are different models to effectively acquire e-resources and sometimes institutions have to reinvent the wheel to satisfy local authorities, clients and needs. Two prevalent methods of acquiring e-resources are:

Acquiring for your own library: In the case of a specialised institute when the resource of interest is not available through any library consortia where you can become member, the only way out is to procure it alone. Here you can decide what to buy, how to buy etc. You may also get a chance to locally test the product and get it evaluated by local experts before proceeding with formal purchase. There also exists scope of negotiations regarding price, features and options, perpetual access of content for licensed period, etc.

Acquiring through library consortium: Consortium promises economy of scale that is tempting for many libraries interested in developing a rich collection of e-resources cost effectively. The price you get for a resource when you subscribe it alone is far higher than the price negotiated by a consortium backed up by the combined strength and collective business potential of many libraries. The consortium may also negotiate for user training, perpetual access, data backup, freebies like you get 1000 journals fort the price of 100 (though no one considers many of those 900 have very few users in the institution) etc.

Both approaches have their own merits and limitations. There is no rule of thumb to say which one is better and which one should be adopted. It is always better to have an informed decision on a case to case basis.

4. STEPS IN ACQUIRING E-RESOURCES

Identifying potential e-resources : Getting a preliminary recommendation from teachers, researchers, students and other members of the user community about any specific e-resource. Alternately, out of survey from other libraries and trade parties like aggregators or agents, identify e-resources of interest to the institution. Seeking recommendation for purchase based on free trial access of products available in the market is also another possibility when you are not very sure of the wide ranging user interests.

Deciding to procure from whom : Printed sources whether you procure it from publisher, distributor or reseller, you get the same content. This cannot be guaranteed with e-resources. To give allowances to exclusivity of current items followed by some publishers and embargo, it is always appropriate to license core resources through publisher and non-core ones through aggregators for better pricing. Ensure about access of current issues and no embargo on content access especially for core e-resources.

Effecting a trial : Ideally, no e-resource should be procured without availing a trial or user evaluation. The pre-subscription free trial facility is normally honoured by most of the publishers, aggregators or trade partners, though some need persuasion on the part of library to comply. The trial serves essentially two purposes: helping the user community to make an informed decision on the use or otherwise of one or a set of e-resources and facilitating the librarian to monitor the interest in the resource by the user community apart from gauging the extent of its coverage and user friendliness of its search interface.

Subscribing or licensing : Library may proceed with the formalities of procuring the e-resource either alone or through consortium based on the constructive evaluation feedback provided by the user community during trial. There are different modes of procuring like onetime fee or through annual subscription. It is always pragmatic to choose a payment option which is cost effective. With specialisations constantly varying in many institutions, it is not advisable to opt for long term purchase options as you can still maintain your access live by paying a nominal fee annually. There should not be any denial of access of content for which the library paid once and later not renewed. Negotiations and licensing agreement should guarantee perpetual access and clearly spell out library's access options in the event of non-renewal of a resource. The providers should either guarantee access to content for which subscription was paid on charges of nominal annual maintenance/ authentication fee or data backup through offline storage. Library should consult other libraries, consortium authorities and finance experts before selecting a particular licensing/subscription option. Inclusion of administration and finance officers in the negotiation committees with trade parties help to eliminate violation of local procedures, include enough checks for advance payment as well as access commitment on the part of suppliers, and ensure faster processing of bills. Libraries are habituated with genuine concerns about meeting user satisfaction and hence would always like to own as many information resources as possible. Adopting a pragmatic course of action is however best feasible for present day academic libraries considering the diversity of specialisations, limited budgets, and cost as well as vastness of e-resources.

Conducting user awareness and training programmes : Many users may not participate in the pre-subscription awareness sessions. Library should devise a series of training sessions on each of the e-resource procured to reach out to different users at their convenience. Such sessions may be conducted by library staff, representatives or specialists of trade partners etc. There should also be easy to learn self-help training packages available for access on the library website to help any interested user who could not attend the training sessions.

Maintaining helplines : There should be professionals in the library who would be available for help and assistance in case any user faces difficulty in accessing the resources. These staff should also monitor the access facility of e-resources continuously. Changes in local network configurations should be gauged regularly and promptly communicated to publishers about IP/password changes, if any, for uninterrupted access of resources. Library staff should also interact with computer staff to keep the internet access and other library computing infrastructure functioning throughout the working hours (and even 24 hours in case of campuses where students stay) without creating any inconvenience to users.

Monitoring usage : This is the most difficult part in e-resource handling for a library as in many cases they have to rely upon the reports sent by the publisher. There are more complaints to this report like it only provides the number of clicks and all clicks may not be readings. Some institutions thus assessed usage based on the log analysis for publishers IPs from the campus computing facility. Usage is done by users who are many and varied and for any external agency to assess usage has to bear with such limitations. In the case of print books also, we assess usage based on issue reports and books taken out from stacks for reading in the library and for those activities also we can doubt about whether the user actually used the book or not. Usage statistics offer the library some tangible inputs about the trends in usage and provide interesting insights for collection development. Sometimes vocal users raise unnecessary demands and that can be effectively countered with the aid of usage statistics.

5. BEYOND CONSORTIA APPROACH

Libraries consider third law of library science (approaching the different aspects of library from the point of view of information resource, so that a resource may be acquired today to meet future demands also, if not for immediate requirements) in collection development decisions. With the variety and number of e-resources, limited funds and very demanding clientele, libraries cannot be that much luxurious with e-resources. Hence purchase decisions need to be influenced by and oriented towards current user needs. Consortium offers bundled products (multiple resources for minimum cost without seriously considering the local utility of each of the individual titles available) and with librarian's interest to project a large resource base in the local collection, sometimes some e-resources are procured which have few or no takers.

Libraries must judiciously evaluate the titles available with each of the consortia and take an appropriate decision by optimising usage of funds avoiding those resources for which there are no takers. Some duplication of resources in different products and some inclusion of resources in non core areas are welcome in case of significant savings in funds.

6. INFORMATION DROUGHT

Ulrich's Periodicals Directory, the most comprehensive source of print and electronic serials data lists more than 300,000 serials from 90,000 publishers covering 950 subject areas and 200 languages. The author could not ascertain the number of refereed serials in the directory from its website. It is not clear whether our country has at least one copy of all the refereed serials. With consortia enabled access leading to many thousands of journals, still there is a possibility that some journal article of interest to users is not accessible leading to information drought. We have to revive Documentary Delivery Service (DDS) channels and register with publisher/aggregator/third party sources for article access (pay per view). There should be some allocation in the library budget with convenient disbursal procedure (such as a certification from the user about the receipt of article with a bill/payment note from the supplier) so that any resource of interest to user community may be availed through such modes. Information plays a key role in research and availability of e-resources with an article procurement utility would significantly improve the quality and visibility of our research.

7. PROBLEMS AND PROSPECTS

Problems are many with e-resources for our libraries but we have to find ways and means to overcome those problems as the prospects are too many.

Librarians face a plethora of problems in dealing with e-resources because many of these are still in the evolving stage and due to the peculiarities of constantly advancing computer technology. There is nothing tangible to show during subscriptions and after the expiry other than user access reports may be baffling for local administrators who are habituated with accession number cross checking or issue receipt reports while clearing or adjusting library bills.

The constant threat of products may be bundled at better prices at a later stage severely influencing current purchase decisions. Main problem with e-resources faced by many libraries are cost effective availability of resources in core areas. Quality is not cheap and we cannot create quality by opting for quantity.

E-journal over its years of existence and use combined with selective access of articles normally adopted by a user for journal has made it a very stable product with options for browse, copy and print. Many of the e-book products are still evolving and struggling to reach the acceptability of users and libraries mainly due to the inherent differences in access and usage of a book and journal. Unnecessary profit oriented restrictions on copying and printing of some e-book products discourage serious users. In case of products with fewer restrictions, price of the product is usually not appealing to libraries. Lack of interest of consortia due to varied interest of books among member libraries and hence absence of consortia discounted prices has so far kept e-books still out of reach of even the best libraries in the country.

Sometimes you drop a print journal seeing its inclusion in an e-resource much against your wishes due to authorities' demand for budget optimisation. One fine morning you find that only old issues are available and sometimes even the journal itself is not figured in later years. Aggregators lease out content from publishers and sometimes negotiations broke in later years leading to elimination of some in the platform. Publishers also charge heavily for new content as they have an interest to exclusively market fresh content leading to an embargo (a trade jargon coined to polish the denial of content access to libraries and users) in coverage through aggregators.

Careful selection and thorough evaluation of e-resources along with aggressive negotiation of prices, features, facilities etc., play crucial constructive roles in enabling e-resource access in our libraries. Allocation for e-resources in many libraries is very minimal causing most to ignore even vital resources is another difficulty and centralised funding of some consortia bailed out many libraries from the budget crunch. Still many institutions and resources remain to be covered through consortia is another limitation.

IT and internet infrastructure are improving consistently in many institutions and still a lot more need to be done to aggressively tap the potentials of e-resources, especially by student users who are often at the receiving end in many libraries. Libraries, computer centres, student hostels all need good power backup facilities to practice 24X7 availability of e-resources for user access.

Library professionals especially by the very nature of their job are very receptive to changes unlike many other streams of professionals in our institutions and hence many are significantly updating their IT skills, sometime on a self learning mode. However stagnation in jobs, lack of incentives, institutional attitude of regarding only library and not rewarding its staff and other such negative tendencies may sometimes force some library staff in libraries not to effectively take part in training and access upkeep of library e-resources.

Conducting the same search on individual search interfaces of different resources may discourage some users and hence there should be federated search facilities to simultaneously search the different resources for easy search experience. Users, many old but few young, have a disinterested attitude to explore the potentials of e-resources to the fullest extent. Some have personal reservations, some are not convinced about the richness of the medium, and some are still too paper centric. Libraries try their best to attract them through publicity, training, awareness etc., and slowly and steadily there are changes in the attitude of such users.

Prospects of e-resources are much written and many said like quick availability (e-format gets uploaded on the site when the computerised typeset version goes to the press), less storage, ease of search/browse/access, ability to incorporate multiple media and formats like audio, video, figures, simulations, computer programmes, executables etc., cost effective mode for purchase/access, easy to link/hyper link with other resources in contrast to the linear text of print resources, easy to cite and quote in own research, surveying and incorporating more relevant resources in teaching and research in less time, avoiding duplication in research due to exhaustive survey of published research, citing more relevant resources in own research paper leading to its acceptance for publication in best journals giving it more visibility, etc. It has also enhanced the access base of resources in libraries as the best of libraries in our country are able to access more journals in electronic form, in some cases 10-50 times their print journals. E-resource access is a great leveller as INDEST consortium guaranteed almost equal number of e-journal access for IITs and NITs when their print journal holdings had wide disparity. The same is the case with Central Universities, better funded state universities and poorly funded state universities as a result of UGC INFLIBNET Centre's Infonet consortia. Through e-resource access, there is no preferred library as every library has access to a similar large resource base helping developing countries to provide equal scope for all its citizens to tap the wider information base for broader education, frontier research and thereby social and community development.

8. HYBRID LIBRARY

E-resources made their strong presence felt in our libraries in the last two decades or so and their dependence would continue to increase. We cannot turn blind eye to such a functional and user centric carrier of information for long time. Library budget of important libraries now have a separate head for e-resources and the allocation in this head is constantly rising. In the case of journals, many serious researchers now prefer the e-version over the print version due to the above virtues of these resources. Earlier users browse the bibliographic databases to identify potential journal articles and availed photocopies. Now with e-resources and alert facilities they can identify, download and print these articles. There are libraries dropping print journal subscriptions for e-journal access as a result of user preferences and institutional demand.

How the user base would respond to e-books may take some time to predict considering the difference in usage of books from journals. But with higher education monographs and conference proceedings procured in more numbers in libraries have many similarities to journal articles and users may adopt a similar interaction with such e-books. In the case of other books which are read in continuity with many pages and chapters or those which are read cover to cover, the availability of e-book readers having new functionalities may attract many readers. Who knows libraries in future may keep e-book readers for issuing to users who are hesitant in buying one on their own.

May be mobile handset based access of e-resources

may emerge in future. May be e-resources will replace print resources in the time to come. In short, today's libraries are more interested in satisfactorily meeting, of course in a cost effective manner, the information needs of their users without creating much distinction in the type, format or other extrinsic characteristics of collection. They are more interested in the intellectual nature of content, irrespective of print or non print, electronic or other storage media leading to the transformation of our libraries as hybrid libraries supporting every aspect of library operations supporting multiple formats and media.

9. INFORMATION EXPERIENCE

E-resources are the most nascent entity in libraries considering the long interaction libraries had with print books or micro media. 15-20 years is too short a period to judge them. The indications are that library's dependence on e-resources is going to continuously increase day by day stimulated both by market forces and user demands. Libraries are no doubt going to amass a huge resource base through this route. Library professionals are going to gain new experiences and expertise making them better performers in academic libraries improving their visibility from passive to active as well as backend to front end. Users are the greatest beneficiaries as they can sift through anything under the sun, in few key strokes. Their information experience has never been so fulfilling and interactive.

REFERENCES

Ulrich's, http://www.serialssolutions.com/assets/publications/Brochure-Ulrichs-Global-Serials-Intelligence.pdf

Tenopir, Carol; King, Donald W.; Spencer, Jesse; Wu, Lei, Variations in Article Seeking and Reading Patterns of Academics: What Makes a Difference?, Library & Information Science Research, vol. 31, no. 3, pp. 139-148, Sept 2009.

Tenopir, Carol; King, Donald W.; Edwards, Sheri; Wu, Lei, Electronic Journals and Changes in Scholarly Article Seeking and Reading Patterns, Aslib Proceedings: New Information Perspectives, vol. 61, no. 1, pp. 5-32, 2009.

Profera, Elyse; Stamison, Christine M., An Agent's Perspective on Issues and Best Practices When Shifting from Print to Electronic Resources, Serials Review, vol. 36, no. 1, pp. 3-9, Mar 2010.

Arora, Jagdish; Trivedi, Kruti, INDEST-AICTE Consortium: Present Services and Future Endeavours, DESIDOC Journal of Library & Information Technology, vol. 30, no. 2, pp. 79-91, Mar 2010.

Noh, Younghee, A Study on Developing Evaluation Criteria for Electronic Resources in Evaluation Indicators of Libraries, The Journal of Academic Librarianship, vol. 36, no. 1, pp. 41-52, Jan 2010.

Cole, Jim; Jones, Wayne (Ed.), E-Serials Cataloging: Access to Continuing and Integrating Resources Via the Catalog and the Web, Haworth Information Press, Binghamton NY, ISBN: 0789017113, 329 pp., 2002.

Peters, Thomas A., What's the use? The value of e-resource usage statistics, New Library World, vol. 103, no.1/2, pp.39-47, 2002.

2

OPEN ACCESS AND PUBLISHERS

1. OPEN ACCESS

Research is done by practitioners in Institutions, funded by Government bodies to a large extent and most of the results get published in scholarly journals, some are published by societies and many published by multinational private firms. Once it is published, the results are not getting accessible to the citizens of the same Government due to copyright restrictions and huge subscription costs of these journals making them out of bounds for many institutions. Free flow of research information irrespective of borders is also required for further research and local applications in crucial areas like medicine. This lead many Institutions and researchers to evolve an alternate model called open access for access outside the conventional stream of restricted access through print and electronic journals offered by regular publishers. 'Berlin Declaration on Open Access to Knowledge in the Sciences and Humanities' clarifies Open Access (OA) contributions must satisfy the following two conditions [1]:

- The author(s) and right holder(s) of such contributions grant(s) to all users a free, irrevocable, worldwide, right of access to, and a license to copy, use, distribute, transmit and display the work publicly and to make and distribute derivative works, in any digital medium for any responsible purpose, subject to proper attribution of authorship (community standards, will continue to provide the mechanism for enforcement of proper attribution and responsible use of the published work, as they do now), as well as the right to make small numbers of printed copies for their personal use.

- A complete version of the work and all supplemental materials, including a copy of the permission as stated above, in an appropriate standard electronic format is deposited (and thus published) in at least one online repository using suitable technical standards (such as the Open Archive definitions) that is supported and maintained by an academic institution, scholarly society, government agency, or other well-established organization that seeks to enable open access, unrestricted distribution, inter operability, and long-term archiving.

Budapest Open Access Initiative (BOAI) defines open access as [2] "free availability on the public internet, permitting any users to read, download, copy, distribute, print, search, or link to the full texts of these articles, crawl them for indexing, pass them as data to software, or use them for any other lawful purpose, without financial, legal, or technical barriers other than those inseparable from gaining access to the internet itself. The only constraint on reproduction and distribution, and the only role for copyright in this domain, should be to give authors control over the integrity of their work and the right to be properly acknowledged and cited."

2 ROLE AND RELEVANCE OF PUBLISHERS

BOAI confirms that open access is economically feasible, gives readers extraordinary power to find and make use of relevant literature, and gives authors and their works vast and measurable new visibility, readership, and impact and suggests self-archiving and publishing in OA journals as two modes to achieve open access to scholarly literature [3].

Wellcome Trust Report made the following observations regarding the dominance of commercial publishers [4]:

- The current market structure does not operate in the long-term interests of the research community.
- Commercial publishers are dominant though many top journals are published by not-for-profit organizations.
- The 'public good' element of scientific work means market solutions are inefficient.
- Electronic publishing is not currently challenging the dominance of commercial publishers.
- Demand is price-inelastic because price is unimportant at point of use for the research community and journals are not easily substitutable for each other.
- Authors face a limited number of journals and their primary concerns are the reputation and reach of the journal. In general, authors are not concerned with price and cost characteristics. There is also a limited amount of substitutability between journals for authors when offering their work for publication.

Peter Suber mentions pricing crisis (libraries must pay intolerable prices for journals) and permission crisis (libraries are hamstrung by licensing terms and software locks that prevent them from using electronic journals in the same full and free way that they may now use print journals) severely impeding research and making libraries paying much more in order to get much less [5]. But the fact is that nobody writes for just keeping their papers in an OA repository, they should also aim for getting peer recognition by publishing in a high impact journal. The author may also try to get his/her paper archived in an OA repository or website along with or after publication in a formal printed journal. The rights and permissions granted by few major publishers are examined here to find out how supportive they are in disseminating research information in a democratic fashion to counter access divide among countries and communities.

2.1. Publishers Studied

The following publishers are examined to find out their tolerance towards open access publishing alternatives:

Table 1. Publishers, Publications and Subject Areas [6-22]

#	Publisher	No. of Journals	Subject Areas
1	Association for Computing Machinery (ACM)	45	Computer Science, Information Technology
2	American Chemical Society (ACS)	36	Chemistry, Chemical Engineering, Chemical Sciences
3	American Physical Society (APS)	10	Physics, Physical Sciences
4	Blackwell	805	Physical Sciences, Life Sciences, Medicine, Social Sciences and Humanities
5	Elsevier Science	1800	Health Science, Physical Science, Life Science and Social Sciences
6	Institution of Engineering and Technology (erstwhile Institution of Electrical Engineers or IEE)	25	Electrical, Electronics, Computers etc.

7	Institute of Electrical and Electronics Engineers (IEEE)	128	Electrical, Electronics, Computers etc.
8	Institute of Physics Publishing (IOP)	58	Physics, Physical Sciences
9	Nature Publishing Group (NPG)	63	Science, Medicine
10	Oxford University Press (OUP)	180	Humanities, Law, Life Sciences, Mathematics & Physical Sciences, Medicine and Social Sciences
11	Palgrave Macmillan	84	Business, Information Technology, Urban design, Statistics, Political Science
12	The Public Library of Science (PLoS)	7	Science. Medicine
13	Royal Society of Chemistry (RSC)	20	Chemistry, Chemical Engineering, Chemical Sciences
14	Science	1	Science
15	Springer	800	Science, Social Science, Medicine, Engineering
16	Taylor & Francis	1000	Arts & humanities, Science, Social Science, Engineering
17	Wiley	2500	Science, Social Science, Medicine, Engineering, Law

3. PUBLISHERS AND OPEN ACCESS

A preprint is defined here as un-refereed author version of the article and a postprint as the final draft author manuscript as accepted for publication, following peer review, without the publisher's copyediting and proof correction process. The responses of the individual publishers towards OA are highlighted in Table 2.

Table 2. Publishers and Open Access [6-22]

#	Publisher	Response to OA
1	Associati-on for Computing Machinery (ACM)	Grants right to post author-prepared versions of the work covered by ACM copyright in a personal collection on the Author's Home Page and on a publicly accessible server of their employer. Such posting is limited to noncommercial access and personal use by others, and must include the following notice both embedded within the full text file and in the accompanying citation: "© ACM, YYYY. This is the author's version of the work. It is posted here by permission of ACM for your personal use. Not for redistribution. The definitive version was published in PUBLICATION, {VOL#, ISS#, (DATE)} http://doi.acm.org/10.1145/ nnnnnn.nnnnnn"
2	American Chemical Society (ACS)	ACS does not permit published or unpublished papers to be posted on Web sites other than ACS's Web sites. On the Copyright Status Form, authors and their employers are informed that they may post on the Web, the title of the paper, abstract (no other text), tables, and figures of their own papers on their own Web sites. In addition, authors may transmit to up to 50 colleagues their own paper, with a notice of copyright and that they alert their colleagues that they may not further disseminate/publish the paper. In addition, authors of new papers are given instructions on how to link to ACS's Web site and the first 50 people who access the article may do so without charge.Students and guides should be aware that posting of theses and dissertations material on the Web prior to submission of material from that thesis/ dissertation to an ACS journal may affect publication in that journal. Whether Web posting is considered prior publication may be evaluated on a case-by-case basis by the journal's editor. If an ACS journal editor considers Web posting to be "prior

		publication", the paper will not be accepted for publication.
3	American Physical Society (APS)	The author or the author's employer can use all or part of the APS published article, including the APS-prepared version (e.g., the PDF from the online journal) without revision or modification, on the author's or employer's website as long as a fee is not charged. If a fee is charged, then APS permission must be sought. In all cases, the appropriate bibliographic citation and notice of the APS copyright must be included.When a fee is imposed on free access e-print server, the author must either obtain permission from APS or withdraw the article from the e-print server or Institutional Repository.The author has the right to post and update the article on a free-access e-print server using files prepared and formatted by the author. Any such posting made or updated after acceptance of the article for publication by APS shall include a link to the online abstract in the APS journal or to the entry page of the journal. In all cases, the appropriate bibliographic citation and notice of the APS copyright must be included. If the author wishes to use the APS-prepared version (e.g., the PDF from the online journal) on an e-print server other than authors' or employer's website, then APS permission must be sought. The author is permitted to provide, for research purposes as long as a fee is not charged, a PDF copy of his/her article using either the APS-prepared version or the author prepared version.
4	Blackwell	Author retains the following rights to re-use the Article, as long as no commercial purposes are involved. Prior to acceptance: We ask that as part of the publishing process Author acknowledges that the Article has been submitted to the Journal. Author can share print or electronic copies of the Article with colleagues; Author may post an electronic version of the Article on personal website, on

		employer's website/repository and on free public servers in his/her subject area. After acceptance: With appropriate acknowledgement to the Journal, the author can share print or electronic copies of the Articles with colleagues, author may post an electronic version of the Article on personal website, on employer's website/repository and on free public servers in the subject area. (For most journals there is a requirement that posting of the Article online does not take place until a specified minimum period has elapsed.)Electronic versions of the accepted article must include the following statement, adapted as necessary for your Article:Author Posting. © {Insert name of copyright holder as shown on the published article}{insert year of publication} This is the author's version of the work. It is posted here by permission of {insert name of copyright holder} for personal use, not for redistribution. The definitive version was published in {insert journal name}, {insert volume, issue number and pages}. http://dx.doi.org/ {insert doi number}Authors are not permitted to post the Blackwell Publishing PDF version of the Article online.Open Access publication option, OnlineOpen enables authors who wish to publish their research in a journal published by Blackwell the opportunity to ensure that their Article is immediately made freely available for all to access online. Here also acknowledgement to the journal source is required and the distribution only for non-commercial purposes. This new pay-to-publish option is an important part of Blackwell's response to the calls for open access and our commitment to viable high quality publishing on behalf of societies. They will be charged the fee when their Article is accepted and the author retains copyright in the Article.
5	Elsevier Science	Author has the right his/her version of the article on personal web page or the web site

		of the institution, provided a link to the journal's home page or the article's DOI is included along with a complete citation for the article. The author can update preprint version (e.g. the Word or Tex form) to reflect changes made during the peer review and editing process.
6	Institution of Engineering and Technolo-gy (erstwhile Institution of Electrical Engineers or IEE)	The author(s) and/or the organisations for whom the work was performed shall be entitled to post preprints of their work (but not the published PDF) on repositories, servers and websites of any sort, provided that these servers are operated by the author's institution or the funding body contributing to the research. Authors may not deposit their article in a third-party repository. Access to such servers is not for commercial use and does not depend on payment of access, subscription, or membership fees.The following wording clearly appears on the front page of the preprint:"This paper is a preprint of a paper submitted to [journal] and is subject to Institution of Engineering and Technology Copyright. If accepted, the copy of record will be available at IET Digital Library". On acceptance, this may be changed to:"This paper is a preprint of a paper accepted by [journal] and is subject to Institution of Engineering and Technology Copyright. When the final version is published, the copy of record will be available at IET Digital Library".The author may also post postprints of their work (reviewed, revised and accepted for publication by the Institution, but not the published PDF) on repositories, servers and websites of any sort, with appropriate copyright notice "This paper is a postprint of a paper submitted to and accepted for publication in [journal] and is subject to Institution of Engineering and Technology Copyright. The copy of record is available at IET Digital Library." The postprint must be the author's version and not the Institution's version/PDF. The postprint must not be posted

		prior to publication of the paper by the Institution and when posted any preprint version should be removed.
7	Institute of Electrical and Electronics Engineers (IEEE)	Authors and/or their companies shall have the right to post their IEEE-copyrighted material on their own servers without permission, provided that the server displays a prominent notice alerting readers to their obligations with respect to copyrighted material and that the posted work includes the IEEE copyright notice.Electronic Preprints. Upon submitting an article to the IEEE for review and possible publication, the author must add the following notice to the first screen of any of his/her previously posted electronic preprint versions of the paper: "This work has been submitted to the IEEE for possible publication. Copyright may be transferred without notice, after which this version may no longer be accessible." When IEEE accepts the work for publication, the author must add the IEEE copyright notice to any previously posted electronic versions of the particular paper submitted and provide IEEE with the electronic address (URL, ftp address, etc.) of the primary electronic posting. When IEEE publishes the work, the author must replace the previous electronic version of the accepted paper with either (1) the full citation to the IEEE work or (2) the IEEE-published version, including the IEEE copyright notice and full citation. Prior or revised versions of the paper must not be represented as the published version.
8	Institute of Physics Publishing (IOP)	Any prior or current availability in electronic form, including but not limited to access as a preprint server on the Internet, has been declared in an attachment before submitting the paper.Any use or publication of the material by the Authors or by authorised third parties shall acknowledge the copyright of the Publisher in an appropriate manner including the complete citation information of the Work as published in the Journal and legend [Journal

		title] © copyright (year) IOP Publishing Ltd.After publication by the Publisher, can be hosted on the Author's personal web site, provided that this is for non-commercial use and that the first page of such use or copy displays the citation information and the Publisher's copyright notice. Where the Author posts the Work to their personal web site then the Author should provide an electronic link to the Journal's web site.To post and update the Work on non-Publisher servers (including e-print servers) as long as access to such servers is not for commercial use and does not depend on payment of access, subscription, or membership fees. Any such posting made or updated after acceptance of the Work for publication shall include the citation information and copyright notice and should provide an electronic link to the Journal's web site.
9	Nature Publishing Group (NPG), A Division of Macmillan Publishers Ltd	Does not require authors to sign away copyright to their articles. Instead, authors provide an exclusive licence and are free to reuse their papers in any of their future published work and on their own website. NPG journals are in World Health Organization's (WHO's) HINARI (Health InterNetwork Access to Research Initiative) scheme which provides free access to public institutions in developing countries. Nature and other NPG journals make selected articles freely accessible to users of SciDev.Net site, further increasing the influence of NPG publications and ensuring that scientists in developing countries can keep up to date with new information.As of January 2005, authors of original research papers published by Nature Publishing Group (NPG) will be encouraged to submit the author's version of the accepted, peer-reviewed manuscript to their relevant funding body's archive, for release six months after publication. In addition, authors will also be encouraged to archive their version of the

		manuscript in their institution's repositories (as well as on their personal web sites), also six months after the original publication.
10	Oxford University Press (OUP)	Prior to acceptance for publication, authors retain the right to make a pre-print version of the article available on personal website and/ or that of employer and/or in free public servers of preprints with acknowledgement that the article has been accepted for publication in OUP Journal. No need to remove preprint versions after publication but these versions should not be updated or replaced with the finally published version. Once an article is published, a link could be provided to the final authoritative version on the Oxford Journals Web site. Where possible, the preprint notice should be amended appropriately.Once an article is accepted for publication, an author may not make a pre-print available as above or replace an existing pre-print with the final published version. Detailed policies on the use of postprints for journals are available at the author self archiving policies link on individual journal homepages.
11	Palgrave Macmillan	Permit authors to archive the final draft of their manuscript (i.e. the version accepted for publication, following peer review and including any resultant revision, but prior to copy-editing by the publisher) on their own website or their institution's or funding body's online repository/archive. But the author's archived version of the manuscript, with proper acknowledgement and a link to the definitive published version on the Palgrave Macmillan Journals web site, must be delayed until 24 months after first online publication in the relevant journal.
12	The Public Library of Science (PLoS)	A complete version of the work and all supplemental materials, in a suitable standard electronic format is deposited immediately upon initial publication in at least one online repository that is supported by an academic institution, scholarly society, government

		agency, or other well-established organization that seeks to enable open access, unrestricted distribution, interoperability, and long-term archiving. To provide open access, PLoS journals use a business model in which expenses of peer review, journal production, and online hosting and archiving are recovered in part by charging a publication fee to the authors or research sponsors for each article they publish.
13	Royal Society of Chemistry (RSC)	PDF of the article can be kept on the personal website(s) of the author(s) or via the Intranet of the organisation(s) where the author(s) works.
14	Science	Permitted to post a copy of the accepted version of the Work on the author's personal website. After the article has been published in Science, authors may post the accepted version (the accepted version of the paper before Science's copy-editing and production) on their personal website on the condition that the reposted article includes a hyperlink to the Work on the Science web site as well as the following notice "This is the author's version of the work. It is posted here by permission of the AAAS for personal use, not for redistribution. The definitive version was published in SCIENCE, {VOL#, (DATE)}, doi:{nnnnn} http://dx.doi.org/{nnnnnnn}".
15	Springer	Author may self-archive his/her version of the article on his/her own website and his/her institution's repository, including his/her final version; however he/she may not use the publisher's PDF version which is posted on www.springerlink.com. Furthermore, the author may only post his/her version provided acknowledgement is given to the original source of publication and a link is inserted to the published article on Springer's website. The link must be accompanied by the following text: "The original publication is available at *www.springerlink.com*". Springer operates a program called Springer Open Choice. It offers

		authors to have their journal articles made available with full open access in exchange for payment of a basic fee ('article processing charge'). With Springer Open Choice, for the growing number of researchers who want open access, Springer journals offer the option to have articles made available with open access, free to anyone, any time, and anywhere in the world. If authors choose open access in the Springer Open Choice program, they will not be required to transfer their copyright to Springer, either.
16	Taylor & Francis	Authors are able to post a pre-print version of the Article on Internet websites including own home page, institutional website or subject pre-print server so long as a link is made on publication to the final published version of scholarly record on the journal's web page.Further, they are able to post, after a 12-month embargo (Science, Technology and Medicine) or 18-month embargo (Social Sciences and Humanities), author's revised text version of the final article after editing and peer review on own home page, institutional website or subject repository so long as a single link is made to the fully reference-linked version of scholarly record on the journal's web page.
17	Wiley	Preprints may be posted as electronic files on the Contributor's own website for personal or professional use,on the contributor's internal university or corporate networks/intranet, or secure external website at the contributor's institution, but not for commercial sale or for any systematic external distribution by a third party (eg: a listserver or database connected to a public access server) with appropriate information about acceptance for publication/ published before and after publication as the case may be with URL link to the journal homepage. The contributor should not update the preprint or replace it with the journal's published version.

Out of the publishers studied, ACS does not permit archiving of preprint or post print of papers. Apart from PLOS, two traditional publishers, Blackwell and Springer provides OA publishing options by making the author or institutions to pay for making the articles immediately available online in other repositories. Some publishers do not permit preprint archiving before publication. Many publishers permit only the authors/institutions/funding bodies to archive the papers restrictively so that their revenues are not affected. Publishers want all the OA archiving to be for non-commercial purposes, generally done with the author versions properly displaying link to the formal version on publisher sites with copyright notice, some even insist for an embargo period so that the content will be exclusively available in their sites for a specific period after publication. The SHERPA (Securing a Hybrid Environment for Research Preservation and Access) -RoMEO (Rights MEtadata for Open archiving) Project of UK identified that 75% of 189 publishers studied formally allow some form of self-archiving of which only 25 % (49) are commercial publishers [23].

3.1. OA Repositories and Journal Output

Table 3 displays how popular is OA archiving in comparison with traditional publication through print journals. Some reasons for not catching up with the print output are archiving has not been done for older publication leaving a substantial percentage of old publications out of these repositories, fine prints and confusing licensing terms by publishers forcing many authors not to explore the OA route to the fullest extent, 'publish or perish' syndrome more dominant than 'archive or perish', etc.

Table 3. Coverage of OA repository with equivalent bibliographic database [24-25]

#	Name of the Repository	Year of Origin	Host Institution	Subject	Content	Coverage of equivalent bibliographic database
1	PubMed Central	2000	National Institute of Health (NIH), USA	Life Sciences	Half a million articles, Around 290 journals	MEDLINE contains over 16 million citations from thousands of life science journals for biomedical articles dating back to the 1950s
2	arXiv.org	1991 in LANL, USA	Cornell University, National Science Foundation	Physics, Mathematics, Computer Science and Quantitative Biology	392,444	9 million records from approx. 4000 journals in INSPEC formed in 1967 with content backdated to 1898.MathSciNet contains over 2 million items dating back to 1864

3.2. OA and India

OA is getting importance in the country due to the following reasons:

Better outlet of local digital library development: Institutional repositories are getting increased attention in the country because of the availability of free software like DSpace and EPrints and institutions getting convinced that archiving their in-house publications for which they own copyright is one pragmatic way to evolve internal digital libraries. Whether populated with many papers published in-house or not, many research and higher education institutions have already engaged in setting up Open Access Institutional repositories.

Largely a consumer than a generator of research information and thirst for research Information: India with many research and educational institutions added at regular intervals eating into meagerly increasing budget is forcing even premier institutions to drop subscriptions to core journals. The consortia based subscription enabled many institutions to at least maintain electronic access to many journals, but still access to quality journals is not available to many of our researchers. Our national output in major international databases is around 2% on the one hand but there is a thirst for research information. Thus it is quite natural that institutions and research personnel wanting research papers published in costly journals, which they can not access through subscriptions/consortia access in their Institutions or Interlibrary Loan/Document Delivery channels, to vouch for the OA route.

Role models of OA: Reputed society publishers in the country also demonstrated that OA access to their papers could be achieved without any substantial drop in their printed subscriptions. Arunachalam points out that all 10 journals of the Indian Academy of Sciences, four journals of Indian National Science Academy with back files, Journal of the Indian Institute of Science back to its very first issue published in 1914, Indian Medlars Centre, National Informatics Centre, New Delhi with electronic versions of 22 biomedical journals, Medknow Publications, a small company based in Mumbai, with 10 medical journals are open-access journals [26].

The Directory of Open Access Repositories (*Open*DOAR) listed the first 40 [27] institutions in table 4 and this show the diversity and size of OA repositories in the country. Since one repository the author is familiar with is not in this list, there may be other institutions with repositories left out from the list. Only 19 of these institutions have more than 1000 items out of which only three have more than 5000 resources, eight institutions have collection above 2000 but below 5000 and another eight institutions have collection above 1000 but below 2000. Ten institutions have collection more than 200 but less than 1000, five institutions with collection in between 100 and 200 and seven institutions with collection less than 100. Thus it is evident that populating these repositories with in-house publications is rather slow.

Table 4. OA Repositories in India

No	Institution	Software	Subject	Collection
1	Indian Institute of Astrophysics, Bangalore			1077 items (as on 14/8/2006)
1a	Central Drug Research Institute (CDRI), Lucknow	DSpace	Biology, Biochemistry, Medicine	135 items (as on 09-12-2008)
2	Central Marine Fisheries Research Institute (CMFRI), Cochin	EPrints	Agriculture, Food, Veterinary, Biology, Biochemistry, Ecology, Environment, Medicine	3633 items (as on 22-09-2010)

3	Cochin University of Science and Technology	DSpace	Multidisciplinary	1912 items (as on 10-11-2009)
4	Delhi College of Engineering	DSpace	Science, Technology	326 items (as on 12-05-2009)
5	Guru Gobind Singh Indraprastha University, Delhi	DSpace	Multidisciplinary	129 items (as on 21-08-2009)
6	ICFAI Business School, Ahmedabad	DSpace	Mathematics, Statistics, Business, Economics, Library and Information Science, Management, Planning	171 items (as on 13-03-2009)
7	Indian Agricultural Research Institute, New Delhi	EPrints	Agriculture, Food, Veterinary	82 items (as on 16-06-2010)
8	Indian Institute of Technology, Bombay, Mumbai	DSpace	Multidisciplinary	1657 items (as on 16-04-2010)
9	National Center for Radio Astronomy (NCRA)	DSpace	Physics, Astronomy	84 items (as on 17-03-2009)
10	Indian Institute of Astrophysics	DSpace	Physics, Astronomy	4211 items (as on 17-03-2009)
11	Indian Institute of Horticultural Research	DSpace	Multidisciplinary	160 items (as on 07-01-2011)
12	Indian Institute of Management Kozhikode (IIMK)	DSpace	Business, Economics	290 items (as on 16-05-2008)
13	Indian Institute of Science (IISc), Bangalore	DSpace (theses)	Multidisciplinary	206 items (as on 05-03-2007)
		EPrints	Chemistry, Mathematics, Statistics,	18949 items (as on 04-02-2010)

			Physics, Astronomy	
14	Indian Institute of Technology, Delhi (IITD)	DSpace	Multidis-ciplinary	2141 items (as on 16-05-2008)
15	Indian Statistical Institute, Bangalore Centre (ISI)	DSpace	Mathematics, Statistics	191 items (as on 13-03-2009)
16	Documentation Research and Training Centre (DRTC), Bangalore	DSpace	Library and Information Science	249 items (as on 13-03-2009)
17	Indira Gandhi Institute of Development Research (IGIDR), Mumbai	DSpace	Multidis-ciplinary	193 items (as on 22-06-2009)
18	Indira Gandhi National Open University (IGNOU), New Delhi	DSpace	Multidis-ciplinary	6190 items (as on 27-08-2008)
19	Information and Library Network Center (INFLIBNET), Ahmedabad	DSpace	Multidis-ciplinary	1144 items (as on 10-07-2010)
20	Information Centre for Aerospace Science and Technology (ICAST), National Aerospace Laboratories, Bangalore	EPrints	Mathematics, Statistics, Technology, Mechanical Engineering, Materials	1320 items (as on 16-05-2008)
21	International Crops Research Institute for the Semi Arid Tropics (ICRISAT), Hyderabad	DSpace	Multidis-ciplinary	3399 items (as on 13-01-2011)
22	School of Biotechnology (SBT), Madurai	EPrints	Biology, Biochemistry	21 items (as on 04-02-2010)

	Kamaraj University (MKU)			
23	Mahatma Gandhi University, Kottayam, Kerala	Nitya	Multidis-ciplinary	913 items (as on 30-03-2009)
24	Management Development Institute (MDI), Gurgaon	DSpace	Multidis-ciplinary	325 items (as on 29-09-2008)
25	National Centre for Catalysis Research (NCCR), Indian Institute of Technology, Madras, Chennai	EPrints	Chemistry, Chemical Technology	1478 items (as on 04-02-2010)
26	National Chemical Laboratory (NCL), Pune	DSpace	Chemistry, Chemical Technology	407 items (as on 13-03-2009)
27	Bibliographic Informatics Division, National Informatics Centre (NIC), New Delhi	EPrints	Medicine	2412 items (as on 05-06-2009)
28	National Institute of Immunology (NII), New Delhi	EPrints	Biology, Biochemistry	10 items (as on 24-10-2008)
29	NICMAS (NIO library), National Institute of Oceanography (NIO), Goa	DSpace	Science, Technology, Arts, Humanities	3763 items (as On 02-02-2011)
30	NISCAIR (National Institute of Science Communication and Information Resources), New Delhi	DSpace	Multidis-ciplinary	504 e-books (as on 04-03-2010) 2020 journal articles (as on 10-11-2008)
31	National Institute of Technology,	DSpace	Chemistry, Chemical	653 items (as on 16-05-2008)

	Rourkela (NITR)		Technology, Physics, Astronomy, Mechanical Engineering, Materials	
32	National Metallurgical Laboratory, Jamshedpur	EPrints	Chemistry, Chemical Technology, Technology	1419 items (as on 15-09-2010)
33	Institute of Petroleum Management, Pandit Deendayal Petroleum University (PDPU)	DSpace	Multidis-ciplinary	64 items (as on 17-11-2010)
34	Raman Research Institute, Bangalore	DSpace	Physics, Astronomy	3568 items (as on 13-03-2009)
35	Sardar Vallabhbai National Institute of Technology (SVNIT), Surat	EPrints	Technology	14 items (as on 26-09-2008)
36	Thapar University (TU), Patiala	DSpace	Multidis-ciplinary	938 items (as on 29-10-2009)
37	The Institute of Mathematical Sciences, Chennai	EPrints	Mathematics, Statistics	41 items (as on 16-04-2010)
38	University of Delhi, Delhi	EPrints	Multidis-ciplinary	170 items (as on 13-03-2009)
39	University of Mysore, Mysore	DSpace	Multidis-ciplinary	5480 items (as on 20-10-2009)
40	Vidya Prasarak Mandal, Thane, Mumbai	DSpace	Multidis-ciplinary	411 items (as on 19-01-2011)
41	Indian Institute of Technology, Kharagpur	DSpace	Multidis-ciplinary	1000 items (as on 4/2006)

4 PROBLEMS AND SOLUTIONS

Consumers than generators want OA repositories: Though there are credible studies about OA giving enhanced visibility and impact of research, researchers are still happy with the conventional route of getting their research published in print journals making such research inaccessible to those who do not have copies of the journal issue. Though a researcher in his/her quest for a particular paper may wish to have a copy in an OA repository, such a wish may not sustain as a practice to archive one's own papers.

Fine prints in Copyright Form: It is true that publishers have become soft on exclusive rights of articles due to the changing times, but they still need their dominance on content published. When authors are required to sign lengthy copyright transfer/assignment forms as a prelude to publication, they get a bit cautious about exploring alternate delivery channels. What is required is to arrive at a general framework irrespective of publishers through which the author/institution/subject specific repository can archive all publications of concern.

Lack of formal channels: Though Institutions have websites there is no policy to archive publications on such sites due to infrastructure or personnel constraints. Also creating OA needs other technical and manpower resources which are not at the reach of many institutions. Identifying library of the institution to collect and archive all in-house publications though an OA compliant repository would help focus and streamline the course of open access archiving in the country.

Discussion Forums and Technical Help: Free software needs more effort to sustain them in individual institutions. You can always fall back upon the software vendor in case of problems with the working of purchased software and we can not get such an advantage in the case of the e-repository software like DSpace or Eprints.

Institutions have either to develop internal expertise or seek the same from volunteers to sustain and stabilize their working in individual sites. There has been a recent spurt of training programmes on repository development software in the country and such programmes can be deemed as great success only if they end up in repository development by the participants.

Beginning is as important as sustaining: The less number of items in the repositories quoted in Table 4 indicates that those who started the repository with much fanfare have difficulties in uploading content due to different reasons. Institutional policies, support, staff, training programmes, user awareness etc. are all required for sustaining a repository.

5. SUSTAINING OPEN ACCESS

OA has emerged as the big bang of digital library development in the country with institutions getting seriously addicted to creating OAI compliant repositories using Eprints/ DSpace in their sites hosting research papers and other in-house publications. Out of the thirteen publishers studied, other than one, all permit some sort of archiving though all publishers wanted to hold on to their supremacy in the content they publish. Apart from PLOS which is an OA Publisher, two conventional publishers have evolved OA publishing models and may be sooner or later all publishers follow suit. But this alternative may not be viable for fund starved authors in the country who have to pay for publishing. Though there are strong tangible advantages of OA publishing and there are many OA journals and repositories, it needs to be studied why OA repositories are not populated like output in printed journals and bibliographic databases. Of the few institutions studied for their repositories, there is no match between the content they publish and content they archive. Perhaps entrusting a unit like library in this venture supported with enough funds, technology and manpower may help the institutions to get strong on OA making the country's research more visible and better disseminated.

REFERENCES

1. Berlin Declaration on Open Access to Knowledge in the Sciences and Humanities, http://www.zim.mpg.de/openaccess-berlin/berlin_declaration.pdf
2. http://www.earlham.edu/~peters/fos/boaifaq.htm#impact
3. http://www.soros.org/openaccess/read.shtml
4. Wellcome Trust. Economic analysis of scientific research publishing, revised edition 10/2003, http://www.wellcome.ac.uk/assets/wtd003182.pdf
5. Suber, Peter. Removing the Barriers to Research: An Introduction to Open Access for Librarians, http://www.earlham.edu/%7Epeters/writing/acrl.htm
6. Association for Computing Machinery (ACM), http://www.acm.org/pubs/copyright_policy/
7. American Chemical Society (ACS), http://pubs.acs.org/copyright/learning_module/module.html
8. American Physical Society (APS), http://forms.aps.org/author/copyfaq.html
9. Blackwell, http://www.blackwellpublishing.com/bauthor/faqs_copyright.asp
10. Elsevier Science, http://www.elsevier.com/wps/find/authorshome.authors/copyright#whatrights
11. Institution of Engineering and Technology (erstwhile Institution of Electrical Engineers or IEE), http://www.iee.org/Publish/Support/Auth/authproc.cfm
12. Institute of Electrical and Electronics Engineers (IEEE), http://www.ieee.org/web/publications/rights/copyrightpolicy.html
13. Institute of Physics Publishing (IOP), http://authors.iop.org/atom/help.nsf/0/F20EC7D4A1A670AA80256 F1C0053EEFF?OpenDocument

14. Nature Publishing Group (NPG), http://npg.nature.com/npg/servlet/Content?data=xml/05_news.xml&style=xml/05_news.xsl
15. Oxford University Press (OUP), http://www.oxfordjournals.org/ access_purchase/publication_rights.html
16. Palgrave Macmillan, http://www.palgrave-journals.com/pal/authors/rights_and_permissions.html
17. The Public Library of Science (PLoS), http://www.plos.org/oa/definition.html
18. Royal Society of Chemistry (RSC), http://www.rsc.org/AboutUs/Copyright/WhatisCopyright.asp
19. Science, http://www.sciencemag.org/about/authors/prep/lic_info.pdf
20. Springer, http://www.springer.com/east/home/materials?SGWID=5-10041-70-1048382-0&detailsPage= journal|copyrightInformation
21. Taylor & Francis, http://www.tandf.co.uk/journals/copyright.asp
22. Wiley, http://www3.interscience.wiley.com/authorresources/ getting-started-faqs.html#copyassign
23. http://www.sherpa.ac.uk/romeo.php?stats=yes
24. http://www.pubmedcentral.nih.gov
25. http://arxiv.org/
26. Arunachalam, Subbiah. India's march towards open access, 5 March 2004, http://www.scidev.net/content/opinions/eng/indias-march-towards-open-access.cfm
27. http://www.opendoar.org/countrylist.php?cContinent=Asia#India

3

Library Services for Distance Education

1. INTRODUCTION

The Distance Education system in the country comprises of a national Open University, 13 state open Universities and 119 distance education directorates attached to traditional affiliating or campus based universities. They altogether offer 500 programmes (5000 courses) to 20 lakhs students through 5000 study centers and 65000 academic counselors.

In a developing country like ours with education emerging as a great leveler to overcome the barriers of caste, creed and poverty, higher education is not at the reach of many. The demand for higher education in the country is increasing by 15% to 17% every year whereas conventional institutions can at beast take only 7% of this load. Thus distance education emerges as a viable option to reach out a large number of learners who are otherwise bereft of the boons of education. Out of the distance education providers, Indira Gandhi National Open University (IGNOU) currently contributes to over 25% of the Country's education and this will be enhanced to over 40% in the 11th plan period.

ILA 'Guidelines for Library Services to Distance Learners' [1] argues that traditional library services designed for on-campus users will not meet the requirements of distance learners. According to Association of College and Research Libraries' 'Guidelines for Distance Learning Library services' [2], "members of the distance learning communities are entitled to library services and resources equivalent to those provided for students and faculty in traditional campus settings". Brophy summarises the basic premise of offering library services to distant users as "Every user, regardless of his or her physical location, should be able to use all library services" [3]. Watson suggests that the library and information needs of distance students do not differ in principle from the needs of their on-campus peers and what differs are the modalities that information providers must adopt [4].

2. DISTANCE EDUCATION

Distance education is characterised by [5]:

- the quasi-permanent separation of teacher and learner throughout the length of the learning process
- the influence of an educational organization in the planning and preparation of learning materials and in the provision of student support services
- the use of technical media; print, audio, video or computer, to unite the teacher and learner and carry the content of the course
- the provision of two-way communication so that the student may benefit from or even initiate dialogue
- the quasi-permanent absence of the learning group throughout the length of the learning process so that people are usually taught as individuals and not in groups, with the possibility of occasional meetings for both didactic and socialisation purposes

It has emerged as a cost effective alternative in offering educational avenues to a large number of population in the developing world. It could also offer a boost to many careers by providing learner centric opportunities in furthering one's educational qualifications and career potentials. Some indices on education in the country compiled from different sources are summarised in table 1.

Table 1. Education and India [6-9]

1	Area	3287263 Sq. Km
2	Districts	599
3	Villages	656975
4	Density of population	324
5	Population (2001 Census)	Male: 532156772 (71.71% rural, Literacy rate: 75.26)Female: 496453556 (72.69% rural, Literacy rate: 53.67)Total: 1028610328 (72.18% rural, Literacy rate: 64.84)
6	Recognised Educational Institutions in 2004-05	407 Universities/Deemed Universities/Institutes of National Importance
7	Higher Education Enrolment (2004-05) as on 30-09-2004	Boys: 7135720 Girls: 4641576 Total: 11777296
8	% of Education Expenditure to GDP (2004-2005)	3.68
9	Total Budget (Rs. in crore)	States/UTs: 433162.91 Central: 386069.00 Total: 819231.91
10	Expenditure on Education (Rs. in crore)	States/UTs 83426.97Central: 21139.03Total: 104566.00
11	Projected Population as on 01-03-2004 (in crore)	107.91
12	Per Capita Expenditure on education(in Rs.)	969.00
13	% of Expenditure on Education	12.76
14	Annual addition of graduates	2 million
15	Annual GDP Growth rate	9%

3. DIGITAL SERVICES AND DISTANCE EDUCATION

The distance education has to surpass the major absence of classroom where the interaction of teacher and learners takes place in regular mode of education with the help of a host of various techno education options. Some of these options other than the printed course materials, face to face counseling and practical training include offline and online audio and video media, broadcasting through radio, television and web, teleconferencing, web cast, web resources, digital libraries, learning portals etc.

Distance education is not class room oriented teacher centric learning but it is learner centric where a teacher/ counselor is one of the media like other tools used in fulfilling the learning needs of the learner. Unlike other media, digital media has several advantages that are inherent to digital domain such as versatility, usage in synchronous/ asynchronous mode, guaranteed availability of 24 X 7, possibility to mix and match text, audio, video, images, simulations, programming etc., ability to share and reuse in a variety of learning contexts, easiness to record, copy and archive with other intellectual assets of the institution etc. There is no wonder why such a media has found wide adoption and multiple applications in educational organisations in general and distance learning institutions in particular.

3.1. Digital Services

It is now more evident that digital services penetrate much faster than the print based services in a more economical way. Thus off-campus library services the world over are looking forward to increasing applications of ICT enabled library services utilizing networked electronic resources. There are guidelines from various associations such as ACRL and ILA detailing the essentials of outreach library services.

3.1.1. ACRL Guidelines

Association of College and Research Libraries (ACRL) Guidelines prescribe that library services offered to the distance learning should meet effectively a wide range of informational, bibliographic, and user needs, such as:

- reference assistance;
- computer-based bibliographic and informational services;
- reliable, rapid, secure access to institutional and other networks, including the Internet;
- consultation services;
- a program of library user instruction designed to instill independent and effective information literacy skills while specifically meeting the learner-support needs of the distance learning community;
- assistance with and instruction in the use of nonprint media and equipment;
- reciprocal or contractual borrowing, or interlibrary loan services using broadest application of fair use of copyrighted materials;
- prompt document delivery, such as a courier system and/or electronic transmission;
- access to reserve materials in accordance with copyright fair use policies;
- adequate service hours for optimum access by users; and
- promotion of library services to the distance learning community, including documented and updated policies, regulations and procedures for systematic development, and management of information resources.

3.1.2. ILA Guidelines

Indian Library Association (ILA) 'Guidelines for Library Services to Distance Learners' stipulate the following services to meet the information needs of distance learners:

- Reference services in person or through telephone/fax/email
- Manual and computerized bibliographic services to faculty
- Borrowing and reading room facilities
- Book bank services
- Mobile library services
- Document delivery services
- Interlibrary loan services
- Preparation of "readings of articles" or course packs
- Remote access to OPAC, website and networks like DELNET, INFLIBNET
- Password enabled access to online journals and electronic databases
- Learning resource centres at public and private libraries

Both these guidelines call for extending services comparable to that being offered for on-campus students by campus universities for their off campus students also. In the case of open universities and other distance learning providers, they have to benchmark with the campus based facilities as far as provision of library support to distance learners is concerned.

3.1.3. Best Practices in Library Services for Distance Education

We are witnessing a host of best practices in offering functional library services to off campus learners.

3.1.3.1. The Open University, UK [10]:

- The Voyager Library catalogue has personalization features, DDS enabled and has links to the electronic items accessible
- Course web sites with links to the library resources relevant for that course.
- Electronic resources accessible are organized by subject and put as links on the website with information on volumes available for access.
- Personalisation feature called MyOpenLibrary, a customisable web page that identifies the learner and presents the relevant library resources.
- Information literacy tools
- Gateway to quality Internet resources selected and classified to cater to the teaching and research needs of faculty, students and staff
- Special service for research students include web links on funding sources, tutorials and resources on writing project proposals and research papers.
- OpenLearn provides free online learning material taken from the University courses, library related material on information skills and freely available resources. It permits to download, amend, reuse, and share the material with anyone (under Creative Common license).
- Open Research Online is a repository of UKOU faculty research publications and other research output.

3.1.3.2. Athabasca University (AU), Canada [11]:

- Provides online access to more than 23,000 journals, 350 e-databases (full text and bibliographic), and over 50000 e-books
- Apart from own subscriptions, databases are also made available through the Canadian Research Knowledge

Network (CRKN) and through the Government of Alberta funded Lois Hole Campus Alberta Digital Library (LHCADL).

- AUCAT (the library system) offers catalogue of library holdings, access to databases and links to selected Internet sites.
- Access to electronic resources is authenticated through name and student/library number.
- Participates in a number of programs which provide for reciprocal borrowing privileges for faculty, staff, and students
- Provides a range of services to staff and students including lending books and other materials, remote access to journal databases and e-books, interlibrary loans, reference services, and technical support
- The Digital Reading Room (DRR), in-house electronic course reserves system designed to provide students with easy access to required and supplementary course materials that are already in digital form, the system is capable of handling many different formats of materials, including journal articles from subscription databases and multimedia, and is fully searchable, allowing for the reuse of digital objects.
- The Digital Reference Centre (DRC) is a collection of electronic versions of encyclopedias, dictionaries, atlases and maps, directories, almanacs, data and statistical information, and handbooks.
- The Digital Thesis and Project Room (DTPR) is a digital repository of own graduate theses and projects.
- Certain databases are also accessible to alumni
- Electronic resources appear in a variety of formats, including online journal articles, electronic books, audio clips, video clips, and Web sites. Some resources are listed under a "Required" heading and students in

the course are expected to consult these. Materials listed under a "Supplementary" heading are optional, and are included to enhance understanding and encourage further exploration of course topics.

3.1.3.3. Open University of Hong Kong (OUHK) [12]:

- More than 250 electronic databases and 12919 + e-journals (many publishers with exact number of journals not indicated)
- The Electronic Library accessible 24 hours a day, provides resources including full text databases and journals, electronic books, selected free Internet resources, in-house digitized web resources like past/specimen examination papers, course readings and library catalogues. OUHK staff and students can access the resources anywhere at anytime with the help of the required software using user name and password. It can be accessed round the clock every day anywhere from a PC with Internet connectivity and also acts as a channel for users to convey their requests for interlibrary loans, enquiries and suggestions.
- Electronic resources contains about 1,500 electronic resources including databases which cover more than 15,000 full-text titles, subscribed electronic journals, and selected Internet resources.
- E-Text Centre contains more than 16,000 titles of electronic books.
- Provides services such as CD-ROM Databases, Interlibrary Loan with online interlibrary loan services, online searches upon request, User Education Programmes, etc.
- The Electronic Reserve Collection is for the use of OUHK users only with access restricted on User ID and password to search and access OUHK examination papers, reference materials, and OUHK electronic

theses & dissertations.

3.1.3.4. Institutions in the US:

There are around 60 University level institutions offering off campus/distance learning/virtual learning programmes. University of Wisconsin - Platteville claims that they are pioneers in distance education since 1978.

University of Wisconsin - Platteville [13]:

- Users can access online guides, resources, e-books, electronic articles, etc., with UWP username and password
- There is a link for distance education students on the main library page, which explains how to use interlibrary loan, check out materials, and access a reference librarian for assistance with your research questions.
- An archived streaming video of online library orientation is kept on the website

University of Florida [14]:

- Off-campus faculty, staff and students share the same library privileges as local patrons
- Course reserves, library instructions and research assistance for distance learners
- Authentication schemes like GatorLink username and password (an individual's computer network identity) and Gator 1 Card (with an 8 character ID number a 14 digit library number) for requesting materials through interlibrary loan and accessing electronic resources from off-campus

3.1.4. Pragmatic Library Services

Library Services for distance learners should ideally have the following minimum facilities:

- Extending on-campus library facilities like circulation,

reference, Inter Library Loan (ILL) and Document Delivery Service (DDS) to off-campus distance learners

- Off-campus access using proper authentication tools to e-journals, e-books and e-databases subscribed/ licensed by the library
- Institutional repository for in-house resources like research publications, reports, theses and dissertations, course materials, conference and workshop proceedings, in-house journals etc., for disseminating intellectual output of the institution to a wider audience
- Electronic resources subscribed as well as those freely available on Internet need to be classified and hyperlinked to course packs/web pages for the convenience of learners
- OPAC should act as a single window system to search print resources in the local collection and access electronic resources
- Reciprocal borrowing/access arrangements with other academic and research libraries
- Consortia agreements with other institutions for optimizing the cost effectiveness of budget allocated as well as to maximize the number and range of electronic resources licensed
- Displaying proper contact details on the website indicating the different sections and various services so that interested learners may contact the staff for required assistance
- Well designed FAQs on the website so that learners may get details of the collection and services of library to start with
- Library orientation programme in a PPT/PDF file on the website to provide just in time access details of library to the interested learners

- Extending special services to specific category of learners like disabled, students from underdeveloped regions, etc.

4. POTENTIALS OF DIGITAL SERVICES

Open Universities and distance learning institutions have so far tried to reach their learners using print media supplemented by broadcasting technology and counseling sessions. Library services are extended at places near to learners through a network of regional/study centres by providing the print books prescribed for specific courses. Due to budget constraints and the large number of learners, it was often difficult in many cases to maintain multiple copies in tune with what is followed (such as one copy for every 5/10/15 learners) by campus based educational providers. There are also difficulties in ensuring the availability of these books to distance learners due to the paucity of infrastructure and library staff, or other operational difficulties.

In a country with wide varying social and economic disparities coupled with cultural and linguistic barriers, multimedia content broadcasted sometimes help to create more impact than linear printed text. With digital technology, it is easy to store, archive and facilitate selective search and access on demand for broadcast content. The stored video also offers the convenience to the learner to stop/replay/fast forward as per the needs of the individual.

Reaching the distant varied category of distance learners through digital media would be more effective seeing the rapid strides in adopting these technologies by the new learner. Computers, internet and bandwidth have all registered significant improvement in recent times. Many institutions are waking up to the untapped potentials of computer aided instruction. Public libraries and internet cafes are acting as computer providers to learners interested in taking advantage of these tools. Distance learning institutions must facilitate computer and network facilities with sufficient need based electronic resources at the different tiers of libraries so that interested learners are never deprived of these facilities.

The mobile technology has penetrated faster than computer and internet that the distance learning institutions should take advantage of this mode for real time communication between learners, teachers, administrators, institutions, facilitators and other stakeholders.

Institutional repositories attain special emphasis in many countries due to several advantages they offer in hosting in-house intellectual content. Unlike campus based institutions, the repositories of distance institutions can also host course materials which are accumulated in large number by many distance teaching institutions. Apart from this, the repository can also provide access to in-house teaching and research output such as research publications, conference proceedings, research reports, theses and dissertations, question papers, model assignments by students, etc.

There should also be some sort of preserving and conserving of the activities different institutions are doing independently on the e-learning and virtual learning front. This may curtail the duplication of such activities and thereby enhancing the output and achieving streamlining of potential applications. There is also a need for intra and inter institutional collaboration involving experts (from the subject concerned, education, computers, networking, media and library/information science) for firming up digital media for educational goals in the country.

5. ACTION PLAN FOR DISTANCE LEARNING INSTITUTIONS

To synergize these potentials, open universities, distance education directorates and other institutions engaged in distance learning must actively pursue the following:

1. Digitization and digital archiving of educational content as is done by IGNOU through e-Gyankosh project: Institutional archiving helps to share and reuse educational materials and would also assist the learners with real time availability of teaching and reference materials
2. Digital streaming of broadcast content in audio and video formats: Unlike campus based facilities, many of the open universities have broadcast content to support the teaching learning process. Broadcasting content would have problems of selective viewing and may not be at the pace of the learner which could be avoided to a large extent by making these content in a non-broadcasting mode with the aid of digital technology
3. Collaborative arrangements within and among these institutions and also with libraries of campus based and research institutions for providing library facilities in the vicinity of learners. It is high time that like reciprocal arrangements evolved in academic libraries in the UK and USA, libraries in the country should also recognize and extend library facilities to students registered in other institutions/universities.
4. Consortia and e-licensing agreements to further the electronic resource base of distance learners
5. Linkages at appropriate levels with campus based institutions to further the cause of education in general and distance education in particular

6. WAY FORWARD

Education becomes monotonous and not as functional as it should be in the absence of exclusive parallel and lateral reading by learners. Campus based learners get enough teacher and peer support coupled with comparatively better library services to take the learning to that extra high. We should not deprive distance learners of their rightful due of library services and digital media appears to be a great leveler for late starters in the developing world. By networking and collaborative arrangements with the vast array of educational institutions in the country, and by pragmatic application of digital technology and digital media, distance learning institutions can create more functional and most effective learning experience to the diverse spectrum of distance learners. Digital media enabled library services make learning and teaching very effective and sooner or later distance education facilities in the country are waking up to the potentials of e-enabling library support by drawing inspirational paradigms from the campus based facilities in the country and distance learning institutions abroad.

REFERENCES

1. ILA 'Guidelines for Library Services to Distance Learners', prepared by the Sectional Committee on Distance Education, Indian Library Association, New Delhi, 28 July 2001.
2. Association of College & Research Libraries (ACRL), Guidelines for Distance Learning Library Services, June 29, 2004, http://www.ala.org/ala/acrl/acrlstandards/guidelinesdistancelearning.htm
3. Brophy, Peter, Library without walls: from vision to reality in Libraries without walls 2: the delivery of library services to distant users, ed. by Peter Brophy, Shelagh Fisher and Zoe Clarke, London: LA Publishing, 1998, pp.6-13.
4. Watson, Elizabeth F., Distance Librarianship: A Perspective,

in Library Services to Distance Learners in the Commonwealth: A Reader, ed. by Elizabeth F. Watson and Neela Jagannathan, Vancouver (Canada): The Commonwealth of Learning, pp. 9-39, 1997.

5. Keegan, Desmond, The foundations of distance education, London: Croom Helm, 1986, p. 49.
6. MHRD, Annual Report 2006-07, http://education.nic.in/AR/AR0607-en.pdf
7. University Grants Commission, Annual Report 2004-05 selected, as on 31.3.05 (University Grants Commission Annual Report 2004-05), http://www.ugc.ac.in/pub/annualreport/summary.pdf
8. Selected educational statistics 2004-05 (as on 30.09.04), http://education.nic.in/stats/SES2004-05.pdf
9. Ramasami, T., Science Education: At the Core of National Development, 12th Professor G. Ram Reddy Memorial Lecture, Indira Gandhi National Open University, New Delhi, July 02, 2007.
10. Open University, UK, Library, http://library.open.ac.uk/
11. Athabasca University (AU) Library, http://library.athabascau. ca/
12. Hong Kong, Open University of, Library, http://www.lib.ouhk.edu.hk
13. Wisconsin, University of, Platteville, http://www.uwplatt.edu/disted/pages/libAcc. html
14. Florida, University of, http://www.uflib.ufl.edu/distance/

4

DELNET Services for Distance Education

1. INTRODUCTION

DELNET is an offshoot of the trend of creating metropolitan and city based network of libraries for sharing information resources to save the financial, human and infrastructure resources and maximize the usage of information resources. Many of these networks fade into oblivion whereas DELNET gained from strength to strength to spread beyond the borders of Delhi to attract more and more libraries in the developing world. The success of DELNET needs to be studied from library and management angles. Two pivotal services offered by DELNET, ILL and DDS along with electronic access options may benefit distance education significantly.

The distance education system in the country is receiving more patronage from Governments, funding agencies and prospective students. It provides better avenues for a person to achieve success in life by continuously improving one's qualifications while on the job pursuing education at one's own pace and space. It comprises a national Open University, 13 state open Universities and 119 distance education directorates attached to on-campus universities. They altogether offer 500 programmes, 5000 courses to 20 lakhs students through 5000 study centers and 65000 academic counselors.

In a developing country like ours with education emerging as a great leveler for overcoming the barriers of caste, creed and poverty as higher education is not at the reach of many. The demand for higher education in the country is increasing by 15% to 17% every year whereas conventional institutions can at best accommodate only 7% of this load. Thus distance education emerges as a viable option to reach out a large number of learners who are otherwise left out of the boons of education.

ILA 'Guidelines for Library Services to Distance Learners' argues that traditional library services designed for on-campus users will not meet the requirements of distance learners [1]. According to 'Association of College and Research Libraries' 'Guidelines for Distance Learning Library services' "members of the distance learning communities are entitled to library services and resources equivalent to those provided for students and faculty in traditional campus settings" [2]. Brophy highlights that "every user, regardless of his or her physical location, should be able to use all library services" [3]. Watson suggests that the library and information needs of distance students do not differ in principle from the needs of their on-campus peers and what differs are the modalities that information providers must adopt [4].

There is a difference in the way the same course is offered in the campus based and distance modes of education. In the campus based mode of education, lot of information and pedagogy takes place through peer interaction and campus libraries for supplementing the teaching learning process. Since a distance learner has very little interaction with fellow students, teachers and campus atmosphere, the self learning materials are devised with more emphasis on simulating these extra features through in-depth and exhaustive coverage of core and related topics. A look at the self learning materials of BLIS and MLIS course of IGNOU with the syllabus of any campus based university will clearly reveal this aspect. Sometimes, in distance education, previous qualifications are relaxed for certain courses (like a person can directly appear for graduation or post graduation without any previous qualifications or through bridge courses) and this needs the current course to cover the essentials of the previous courses too. Thus a distance learner needs background materials for core and related topics and sometimes more library support than what is offered to regular students. The present library support system can not afford to provide anything comparable to the campus based mode of education and network facilities like DELNET would be the natural choice to supplement the library support currently offered to distance learners.

2. DELNET

DELNET began its operation in January 1988 under the support of the then National Information System for Science and Technology (NISSAT), Department of Scientific and Industrial Research, Government of India. It was registered as a society in 1992 and is currently being promoted by the National Informatics Centre, Department of Information Technology, Ministry of Communications and Information Technology, Government of India and India International Centre, New Delhi. It attempts to promote resource sharing among the libraries through the development of a network of libraries. It aims to collect, store, and disseminate information apart from offering computerised services and coordinated efforts for suitable collection development thereby reducing unnecessary duplication wherever possible.

It has already created union databases of books, periodicals, CD-ROMs, articles, audio and video, theses and dissertations available in member libraries (see Table below). All these databases run on DELSIS, an in-house software developed on BASISPlus. It provides ILL, DDS, retro-conversion, reference services, apart from offering technical support to member institutions in the selection of hardware, software, communication links, database creation; and in resolving technical problems faced by member-libraries.

Table: Quantitative Aspects of DELNET [5]

Sl. No	Feature	Value
1	Union CataLogue of Books	53,95,778
2	Union List of Current Periodicals	25,252
3	Union Catalogue of Periodicals	20,235
4	Databases of Periodical Articles	8,88,342
5	CD-ROM Database	2,281
6	Union List of Video Recordings	5,000
7	Union List of Sound Recordings	748
8	Databases of Theses and Dissertations	44,304
9	DEVINSA Database	20,000
10	Members	India 1129 (Delhi- 177, Andhra Pradesh- 115, Maharashtra- 111, Tamil Nadu- 160, Uttar Pradesh- 97, Karnataka- 92)Outside India 16, Total Members 1145 (More than 70% of these libraries are in science and technology area and around 90% are academic institutions)

3. DISTANCE EDUCATION

Distance education has emerged as a cost effective

alternative in offering educational avenues to a large númber of population in the developing world. It could also offer a boost to many careers by providing learner centric opportunities in furthering one's educational qualifications and career potentials.

Watson proposes the following factors for growth of distance education:

- Phenomenal growth of the world's population leading to an unprecedented need or desire for education at all levels
- Many persons wish to re-tool themselves to accommodate changes in the workplace or a desire for career change
- Career change demands an individual to acquire information, skills, aptitudes and attitudes that are new
- Escalating costs of establishing conventional educational institutions, distance education provides economies of scale in activities and operations
- It countermands some of the negative effects that changes in residential location, either under voluntary or forced circumstances

Association of College and Research Libraries (ACRL) Guidelines quoted in the earlier chapter prescribe that library services offered to distance learning should meet effectively a wide range of informational, bibliographic, and user needs. Similarly the Indian Library Association (ILA) 'Guidelines for Library Services to Distance Learners' stipulates certain essential services to meet the information needs of distance learners. Both these guidelines call for extending services comparable to that being offered for on-campus students for distance learners also.

4. DELNET FOR ADVANCING EDUCATION AND RESEARCH

DELNET should attempt the following for advancing education and research, especially through the distance mode which still has a large untapped potential for turning the country to a pivotal position in the emerging information age and knowledge economy:

1. Proper update of holdings of member libraries at more frequent intervals

The data from member libraries are collected and merged with appropriate holding details for creating the union database by DELNET. Sometimes this process may take time due to the decentralized work procedure adopted. One way to still provide the members about whether a book/ journal they are looking for is available in any of the member libraries of the network is by providing an option to search the individual OPACs or providing an option to search these individually at the DELNET site.

2. Creating a National Union Catalogue/Database

Though not a rich country, we still invest considerable amount of resources for our educational and research institutions and their libraries. Still no one knows what is available where without individually contacting each of these institutions which is a difficult proposition. As a network centre with a track record of creating databases of the order of 5 million records, DELNET should take the lead in creating National Union Catalogue of monographs, back volume holdings of serials, and current serial holdings.

3. Give and Take Options for non Members

Apart from the present option for enrolling as a member by paying the requisite fee for membership and for services availed, DELNET should evolve the concept of non-members to lend materials to DELNET and seek the services based on a charge for individual services received or on a reciprocal basis. This may ultimately benefit the member libraries, enhance the visibility of the network and improve the success rate of meeting ILL/DDS requests and quality of services.

4. Collaborative Arrangements

INSDOC (now NISCAIR) had collaborative arrangements with British Library Document Supply Centre (BLDSC) for document delivery earlier. Similarly the National Centre for Science Information (NCSI) one time had similar arrangements with the National Library of Australia. Even after the successful operation of many library consortia in the country, still there is a demand for journal articles not available in any of the consortia or holdings of the libraries in the country. DELNET should undertake collaborative arrangements with international library cooperatives, library networks, libraries, or trade parties for real time availability of journal articles of interest to the users.

5. Reference Libraries of Books

DDS Services may be fulfilled by collaborative arrangements whereas for ILL services, DELNET should have a chain of libraries with good collection as reference libraries of books for executing this highly popular service. There may be cases where a book on demand is not available in the country at all and DELNET should have a contingency plan to procure a copy. Since setting up a library for this purpose is not advisable, may be some libraries can be identified as the place to maintain these books on a cost sharing basis. As enunciated in ACRL Guidelines that 'reciprocal or contractual borrowing, or interlibrary loan services using broadest application of fair use of copyrighted materials' should be the motto of DELNET.

6. Library Consortia

There are few consortia which are operational in the country for e-journal access such as MHRD-AICTE INDEST (mainly for technology and science, libraries who wish to join on their own can do so for certain resources where publishers do not insist for print holdings), UGC Infonet (largely for UGC affiliated Universities and Colleges), IIM Consortium (for specific journals from certain publishers only for IIMs), CSIR Consortium (science and technology journals of interest to laboratories under CSIR) etc. Still there is scope for more open ended consortia in the country because of the poor print holdings base in many of our libraries. There are also many research libraries which are largely single entities and can not take advantage of any of the existing consortia. As a successful library cooperative, perhaps DELNET can take the lead in framing a library friendly consortium for the benefit of fund starved but information demand overflowed libraries in the country.

7. Electronic Access options

Some of the request under ILL/DDS could be accessed in the electronic format (e-journals, e-books etc.) by purchase/access/licensing rights from publishers/ aggregators/ distributors of information. The future of library and information services lies in looking beyond print only to a print plus electronic access environment. As a trend setter in sharing print resources, DELNET should now take the lead in sharing of e-resources to the fullest possible extent honouring all the valid rights of various stakeholders involved in the information communication process,

8. Repository of Indian Research

Ready availability of free digital library software like DSpace, Eprints and Greenstone and their training and peer support options force many institutions to venture into the setting up of institutional repositories for archiving output of local research and other intellectual artifacts. However in the long run, many small research institutions would not be able to sustain the effort. Being a network centre with reach beyond the borders of the country, DELNET may setup a repository for archiving digital objects of its member libraries. May be the repository should be such that any author/researcher willing to upload their papers would be able to do so easily.

9. Portal Based Services

Many libraries are unable to maintain computer support due to inability to hold computer staff in the library due to better perks elsewhere forcing them to leave at sooner intervals. The centralized computer facility in the Institution may regard computer support to library at a lesser priority than the support to research, academic and administration activities. In this premise, the computer infrastructure of DELNET should evolve portal services for its member libraries willing to outsource these activities. DELNET can host websites of member libraries, archive and serve their digital libraries, 24 hour serving of OPAC of individual libraries etc.

5. CONSTRAINTS AND OPPORTUNITIES

1. Provision for Consistent and Systematic Funding

DELNET still receives meager support from the Government and largely operated through small finances it generated out of memberships and services. Seeing the success rate of its facilities and services, and its impact in the information service scene in the country, it is high time that it be provided with required support and may be elevated as an autonomous institution under Planning Commission/MHRD. DELNET may be able to venture as a catalyst in education and research support only when source of continuous funding is ensured not only to sustain the existing operations but also to venture into newly emerging areas.

2. Reaching out to Distance Education Institutions

The campus based institutions can join DELNET by paying the requisite fee and avail the services for all its clientele. The same is the case for electronic access for campus based institutions offered liberally by publishers/ aggregators. Since distance education institutions practice multi-site delivery, some times they have to shell out extra money for enabling access at the different Regional and Local support centres envisaged. As the distance learning institutions in the country survive to a large extent with limited support from Government and student fees, DELNET should come up with distance education friendly membership options for the entire gamut of support centres under one Open University being served with the network services.

6. INFORMATION SUPPORT

The Distance Education Council, the apex body of distance education, is engaged in a massive modernization plan for information support to distance learners. Equitable information access to distance learners who are always at a disadvantage due to their wide varying intellectual abilities and location throughout the entire geographic reach of the country is now being worked out through consortia, encouraging local digitization efforts, disabled friendly information support etc. As a pioneer in information support for libraries through shared access, DELNET has a stake in enhancing the information support for distance education in the country. The nine point action plan suggested, though some may found a bit ideal, would help in not only enhancing the service spectrum and visibility of DELNET but also evolving better information support for distance learners who in many cases are often pushed to the receiving end.

REFERENCES

1. Indian Library Association (ILA) 'Guidelines for Library Services to Distance Learners', prepared by the Sectional Committee on Distance Education, Indian Library Association, New Delhi, 28 July 2001.
2. Association of College & Research Libraries (ACRL), Guidelines for Distance Learning Library Services, June 29, 2004, http://www.ala.org/ala/acrl/ acrlstandards/ guidelinesdistancelearning.htm
3. Brophy, Peter, Library without walls: from vision to reality in Libraries without walls 2: the delivery of library services to distant users, ed. by Peter Brophy, Shelagh Fisher and Zoe Clarke, London: LA Publishing, 1998, pp.6-13.
4. Watson, Elizabeth F., Distance Librarianship: A Perspective, in Library Services to Distance Learners in the Commonwealth: A Reader, ed. by Elizabeth F. Watson and Neela Jagannathan, Vancouver (Canada): The Commonwealth of Learning, pp. 9-39, 1997.
5. DELNET, http://delnet.nic.in/

5

PRICE VERIFICATION IN BOOK ACQUISITION

1. INTRODUCTION

The most unstable and difficult to correctly ascertain entity related to a book that is purchased in libraries is its price. Earlier the practice of not printing the price in the book concerned has been prevalent in the case of international publishers and now widely followed by many Indian publishers as well. Publishers want to make revisions at consequent intervals on titles printed earlier and that may be the primary reason for not printing the prices in the book. Another reason could be, especially in the case of international publishers, that the same title is marketed in different currencies in different parts of the world, like titles of some international publishers sold in US Dollar in USA, in British Pound in UK, and in Euro in other parts of Europe. In the pre-Web era, these price revisions have to wait for longer periods due to the time taken in consolidating and printing catalogues/brochures of books on sale. With web supporting dissemination of information and even holding commerce in a big way, publishers can revise the prices of titles at the click of a button at as many intervals as possible and desirable. Publishers justify operational and warehousing costs as reasons for upwardly revising prices of older titles. Sometimes poor response of a title may also lead to reduction in its cost. These price instabilities affect libraries in the following ways:

- Most of the time, libraries have to spent more funds for procuring titles which they must have procured at lower rates had they acquired those titles earlier
- Libraries in developing countries have to bear the onslaught of not only revision in prices but also the higher rates of exchange for foreign currencies
- Price verification and certification emerging as one of the important activities of the senior staff/in-charge of Acquisition Section
- Lack of standardization in documents submitted by suppliers to substantiate the price quoted for a book making it considerably difficult to certify the price

Since acquisition neither initiates nor completes the process of building an organized collection and deals only with a temporary transaction, the acquisitions departments must frequently meet conditions set by others and is expected to be flexible, adaptable and accommodating to the goals of other units [1]. Libraries follow considerable exercise in allotting the amount allocated for purchasing books into different disciplines, subjects, departments and divisions. Academic libraries should follow a formula for allocating collection development funds and the policy and the budget should be available to faculty, staff, students, and other service populations [2]. However when dealing with the expenditure of this budget, they have limited control over whether the money allocated is being spent judiciously or are they being paid the wrong price for the right book. Cogswell considers fiscal management as one of the key functions of collection management like planning and policymaking, collection analysis, materials selection, collection maintenance, user liaison, resource sharing, and program evaluation [3]. Like allocating budget available on a user convinced formula to different disciplines of interest, carefully verifying the prices of books quoted by suppliers would also form another issue of concern in efficiently managing the acquisition finances.

Review of Previous Studies

The continuously increasing cost of publications and rising foreign exchange rates and the inability of library budgets to keep up with prices are evident and since 1970 most library budgets have decreased but prices have risen by an average of 160% [4]. Guha et al. presents data on the average prices of books in various subject areas and analyses the rise in prices over the period 1971-77 and discusses the impact of price rise with reference to the acquisition of books [5]. Sharma discusses the book pricing techniques adopted by publishers and how rising prices have appreciably affected the collection development pattern [6]. Satyanarayana and Satyanarayana examines briefly the economic factors affecting collection development in university libraries based on book and periodical price trends over the period, 1988-1992 [7]. Bhatt suggests some solutions to soaring inflation, decreasing library budgets, and increases in the price of foreign books and periodicals to augment the acquisition programme in libraries and information centres [8]. Reddy and Suseela identifies the impact of indiscriminate pricing policies of publishers, foreign exchange, mailing charges and inflation on periodical prices [9]. Ismail stresses the influence of frequent rise in prices of books and the problems faced by librarians due to variations in discount, non-printing of prices and other variations in editions in the backdrop of unfair practices of publishers and lack of authentic bibliographical sources to check the original prices [10]. With retailer demands and consumer expectations placing so many pressures on margins these days, Clifford speculates how publishers arrive at the price of a book, anticipate their earnings, or cover their costs [11]. Internet bookselling together with the increase in international travel and the globalization of media coverage made booksellers to suggest publishers to acknowledge this global market and harmonize their book prices accordingly [12]. Book prices appear to be highest in the sciences and technology and publishers appear to be pricing by targeted market [13]. Publishers depend on certain formulae influenced by advances in technology, such as computerised typesetting devices, to decide upon the prices of books [14].

1. PRICES OF BOOKS

The General Financial Rules (GFR) of Government of India Rule 99 granted exemption for "books, publications, periodicals, etc., in a library" from the term 'stores'. Perhaps this may be the reason why libraries or institutions do not insist for the price of books marked in the purchase order to be the same as that billed. In many cases, libraries consider the price of the book at the request/order stage only as an approximation to assess the budget required for purchasing the same and whether it shall be accommodated in the existing budget. The actual price of the book shall be checked at the time of supply with publisher's prices. The correct price of the book can be decided only from the publisher's sources. This was done earlier with the help of publisher's catalogue or publisher's invoice to importers/ suppliers. Not only international, now even many Indian publishers do not display the price of the book in the book and the price may be assessed from the publicity material such as catalogues, brochures, price lists, web site, etc. Though prices of online bookstores like Amazon differ from the publisher's price; many of the publishers display the correct price on their web site. Their sites also contain special offer prices for pre-publication, seasonal discount, etc.

One way to resolve price problems quickly and in accepting ordered books in a faster manner is by considering the price information on the publisher site as the authentic price. The only catch in accepting this is some suppliers who sourced a book at an earlier lower price may claim the revised price with website proof. Many publishers are of the habit of revising their prices annually, semi-annually, quarterly, monthly, or at more frequent intervals to recover their warehousing and operating costs. This may sometimes help distributors and suppliers to claim higher price for a book sourced at the lower price by providing a copy of the revised price list from the publisher. They may also do the same with proof of price to their advantage by producing copies of purchase/import invoices from the Publisher which suit their claim. Trade parties always express difficulties to submit originals of such invoices. Publishers should mark copy number in all books and print this number in their purchase invoices to eliminate any exploitation of one invoice for multiple deals by distributors/sellers/suppliers.

It remains to be seen whether publishers evolve such customer/library friendly measures causing unhappiness to their trade fraternity. Though difficult to eliminate such unfair trade practices, but can be prevented to some extent by always insisting for import invoice from the publisher. This may also help to weed out books brought to the country through doubtful means without proper import documents. Another way to eliminate the burden of price revisions in between requisition, order and supply stages is by entering into a contract with the supplier, taking the publisher price at the time of ordering as authentic and issue the purchase orders with a condition that 'no further increase of the price acceptable hereafter'. But the library will be a loser in few cases where the publisher reduces the price of a book due to the unpopularity or overpricing of a particular title. Being social service institutions and as active partners in the scholarly information communication chain, it is not difficult to involve suppliers as partners in this pious role of libraries by taking them into confidence and asking them to work in 'no more increases in prices in between but reductions are always welcome' approach.

2. CASE STUDY

The Central Library of the Indian Institute of Technology, Kharagpur has probably one of the finest collections of monographs and serials in premier areas of science, engineering and technology in the country. Acquisition Section of the Central Library, IIT Kharagpur collects requests for books from around 500 faculty members attached to 28 Departments/Centres/Schools of the Institute. The Section gets the required data entered in the LibSys software used for library house keeping operations. It then identifies and places orders for these books with around 40 suppliers, local as well as outstation. On receipt of the ordered books, they were checked and accessioned and transferred to the Technical Processing Section for further processing such as classification, cataloguing, and indexing. The bills of the books accessioned were cumulated in contingent bills and sent to the Central Finance & Accounting Section of the Institute for payment through cheques to the concerned suppliers. The Library purchases two types of books- general (research) books (specialized books of high standard meant for research activities procured in single copies) and textbooks (books prescribed for courses and normally purchased in multiple copies). The status of acquisition budget is provided in Table 1. The details presented in Table 2 give an indication of the professional and administrative work involved, especially because books are ordered right from the first month of the financial year and books as well as bills are processed till the last month of the financial year.

Table 1. Budget Allotted and Spent for Procuring Books

Sl. No	Financial Year	Budget Allotted (in lakhs of Rs.) for			Budget (in lakhs of Rs.)	
		Research Books	Text Books	Total Books	Ordered	Spent
1	2003-2004	100	19	119	100.92	56.78
2	2004-2005	104	21	125	141.52	69.73
3	2005-2006	83.50	16.50	100	90.94 (till 10.01.2006)	58.00 (till 10.01. 2006)

Table 2. Status of Acquisition Activities

Sl. No	Financial Year	Orders Placed	Titles Added	Payment Requests Generated	Bills Processed
1	2003-2004	992	3795	292	962
2	2004-2005	560 (till 30.09.2004)	2541 (till 30.09.2004)	230	1319
3	2005-2006			233	1143

The major steps in acquisition operations are as follows:

1. Receiving requisitions from users for purchasing newly published books, reports and theses
2. Checking for eliminating purchase of duplicate copies of books
3. Generating control numbers by making the required basic bibliographic entries in the LibSys software
4. Verifying whether the book recommended can be procured from the budget available for that concerned department/type of book
5. Seeking the approval of recommended non-duplicate

titles from the Departmental Purchase Committee (DPC)

6. Generating order and sanction forms through LibSys
7. Despatching order forms to empanelled suppliers who approved the requisitions and monitoring the status of supply of books ordered
8. Checking supplied books with bibliographic details quoted in the order and for its physical condition, edition etc., as well as accepting the same
9. Assigning Accession Number through the LibSys and completing the Accession Register manually
10. Verifying and certifying prices of books, discount and exchange rates quoted
11. Processing bills for payment
12. Answering any intermediate queries from users, suppliers and administration, and
13. Providing status report and attending to queries about book budget and acquisition activities at any point of time

Out of these, step 4 deals with budget monitoring and step 10 about ascertaining correct prices are quoted by suppliers.

2.1. Terms and Conditions for Purchasing Books

Library purchases books from its empanelled suppliers and all such suppliers are required to follow the prescribed terms and conditions. Some of the terms which are of importance in the context of price certification are extracted below:

Submission of Bill: The Supplier should submit the bill in triplicate mentioning the order no. and date. The Bill should accompany the relevant challan in duplicate and the supporting documents: copy of the original import invoices/ current publishers' catalogue/Publisher's Price list/Price

Proof.

Price Certificate: A price certificate should be incorporated in the bill stating that price quoted is correct.

Exchange Rate: Conversion rate of foreign currencies should be charged as per RBI rate prevailing as on the date of receipt of order.

Discount: The minimum discounts on the books are as under:

General and Text Books:

- 15% (20% if more than 20 copies are ordered) for books published within the past 2 years from the date of the Purchase Order.
- 20% (25% if more than 20 copies are ordered) for books published within the past 2-5 years from the date of the Purchase Order.
- 25% (30% if more than 20 copies are ordered) for books published 5 years before the date of the Purchase Order.

Reference Books:

- 20-25% for books published within the past 2 years from the date of the Purchase Order.

3. IMPORTANCE OF PRICE VERIFICATION

There are five major reasons for the increasing emphasis the library has paid in ascertaining correct prices of books before passing bills of suppliers:

3.1. Shift from uniform discount GOC exchange rate to a variable discount RBI exchange rate purchase system

Till the financial year 2002-2003, the Library was buying books at 10% discount (higher discount was obtained sometimes through negotiations only for expensive reference books) at Good Offices Committee (GOC- Committee presently comprising of different book sellers associations' which fix the exchange rates of foreign currencies on a monthly basis. Most of the time the GOC rates are 3-8% higher than the corresponding bank rates). The discount rate was enhanced to 15% from January 2003 and during the Technology Book Fair 2003 in a meeting with the participating suppliers, it was decided to implement a variable discount of 15% for books published in the last two years, 20% for those published three years prior to that and 25% for those published beyond the last five years (essentially aimed at discouraging suppliers to bring older books). 5% extra discount shall be claimed for textbooks while ordering more than 20 copies and reference books. Currently the exchange rates for foreign currencies are calculated as per rates displayed on the Website of Reserve Bank of India as on the date of order.

3.2. High cost of books purchased by the Library for academic and research activities of the Institute

Table 3 presents the average cost of books purchased by the Library in two successive years. International titles are reprinted at special prices or Rupee prices in fields such as management or computer science having more educational institutions but such a trend is not visible in many other disciplines. There are also not many titles for post graduate level in affordable prices. This forces the Library to buy original editions as text books. The higher the cost of books purchased, the more is the need for stricter norms to verify and check the prices charged for optimizing the acquisition activity and to judiciously follow the purchase and audit norms set forth by the Institute.

3.3. Publishers change distribution zones to bill titles in Pound or Euro after the downswing of Dollar against Indian Rupee

On the one hand publishing is being converted like any

Table 3. Average Cost of Books Purchased

Sl. No	Financial Year	Research Books			Text Books		
		No	Cost (in lakhs of Rs.)	Average Cost	No	Cost (in lakhs of Rs.)	Average Cost (Rs.)
1	2003-2004	1950	56.50	2897.44	1845	3.61	195.66
2	2004-2005	1154	24.41	2115.25 (till 30.09.2004)	1387	8.16	588.32

other big business through acquisitions and mergers forcing all the titles under one publisher to be billed in one currency in different regions. There is also an increasing trend of corporatization of higher education publishing or conglomerates with multiple business arms acquiring publishers and making publishing as a crass commercial activity. Some of the significant mergers to name include Elsevier taking over Academic Press, merging of Springer and Kluwer, and CRC Press, Marcel Dekker etc., coming under Taylor & Francis. There are also distribution regions identified by publishers making titles of many publishers available in India preferably billed in appreciable currencies of Pound and Euro, especially after Indian Rupee registering significant strength against US Dollar in the last few years.

3.4. Variety of supporting documents produced by suppliers to justify the prices charged

The suppliers attach different types of documents such as catalogues, purchase invoice from publishers/distributors/importers etc., to support the prices quoted. Many of these documents are Xerox copies of copies and this forced to doubt its authenticity. The Library after examining the practices prevalent in different Institutions and consulting various experts has arrived at the conclusion that only publisher can fix the price of the book and the supplier has to attach the purchase invoice from the publisher to justify the price quoted. In many cases most of the suppliers failed to provide this document citing various reasons. But to clear the bills in a reasonable time and to spend the funds allocated for purchasing books in a financial year, the Library has arrived at the pragmatic decision of clearing the bills if the price quoted is as displayed on the website of publisher. If the supplier wants to charge a higher price, the company has to produce a copy of the purchase invoice from the publisher on a date after the date of order or else they have to satisfy with the current publisher price displayed on their website. This decision was acceptable to all the suppliers on the panel and this made the Library to continue with the acquisition operations without any delay.

3.5. Administrative Support in DPC

All recommended non-duplicate titles were placed in the DPC for its ratification before releasing formal purchase orders with the empanelled book suppliers. This committee had all Deputy Librarians, In-Charge of Acquisition Section and another Assistant Librarian from the Central Library and Deputy Registrar (Finance & Accounts) of the Institute from Administration or his nominee as its members. The representative of Administration in this Committee always insists that the price of the book quoted by the Supplier at the time of approving/recommending a book should be treated as the maximum price that can be offered for that title and under no circumstance a higher price shall be paid. However to comply with Government norms and audit procedures, the Library should take enough precautions to ascertain that the price quoted is not higher than the prevailing prices stipulated for that title by its publisher.

4. METHODOLOGY USED

While checking the bills for certification for payment, various cases of wrong prices quoted by the suppliers were come to light. These cases are recorded in a register to assess the trends. While checking the prices, some other cases were noticed where suppliers have supplied books at prices lower than the current prices displayed on the publisher sites. May be the prices were changed in between the books are procured from their principals by the suppliers and supplied to the Library or may be there are special prices applicable to the country which are not announced through formal channels. These cases are also recorded separately and present the analysis of savings to the Library for three financial years 2003-2004, 2004-2005 and 2005-2006. The data gathered is presented in tabular form with inferences and discussion.

4.1. Limitations

Since an automated acquisition system also involves considerable time consuming manual tasks, some times the required data could not be entered in the register before certifying bills and hence no exhaustiveness of the data compiled is claimed. However we attempt to draw general inferences regarding prices quoted by suppliers to a premier library, the data collected and presented would suffice the purpose for which it was intended.

Due to many administrative and professional practices involved in acquisition work, all to be conducted in a time bound fashion; the library could not ascertain the publisher's price of the book at the time of order. Prices were checked only at the time of supply of the book while certifying bills and hence do not keep track of those cases where a price change is effected by the publisher in between.

Since commercial interests of suppliers are at stake, their names are not revealed and instead codes are used. It was found that suppliers involved in these cases are many failing to draw any parallel between their performance otherwise and their inclusion here.

Bills with higher publisher prices for the financial year

2005-2006 could not be presented due to operational difficulties in collecting this data.

This discussion does not touch upon the issue of country specific pricing of books in tune with the GDP/GNP of the country and the affordability to its citizens/ institutions or other such issues required for better penetration of books published by international publishers in developing countries.

5. SUPPLIER QUOTING HIGHER PRICES

Table 4.1 lists 116 cases of the financial year 2003-2004 where suppliers have billed for prices higher than the publisher prices at the time of supply leading to a saving of Rs. 116602 to the Library. Suppliers 3 and 15 have 13 bills of price overshoot followed by Supplier 10 with 9, Supplier 28 with 8 cases and Supplier 5 with 7 such cases. There are two suppliers (19 and 29) with six cases, two suppliers (24 and 25) with five cases, and four suppliers (1, 16, 17 and 32) with four cases of bills quoting prices higher than the prevalent publisher prices. Nine suppliers have two cases and seven suppliers have single cases of price overcharge. In one bill of Supplier 28, the Library could achieve a saving of Rs. 8036. Other bills with substantial price jumps with amount (supplier code) details are Rs. 4440 (17), Rs. 4134 (03), Rs. 3985 (15), Rs. 3851 (12), Rs. 3574 (19) and Rs. 3454 (05). There are eight cases from Supplier 28 leading to a price rise of Rs. 19276, 13 bills supplied by Supplier 15 qualifying for a price saving of Rs. 16183 and 13 bills quoting higher prices from Supplier 03 with a price overshoot of Rs. 14784. Other cases worth mentioning in the order of price saving (supplier code, no. of books) are Rs. 9603 (05, 7), Rs. 6898 (10, 9), Rs. 6770 (17, 4) and Rs. 6035 (19, 6). The average price rise for a supplier is calculated as a measure of the total price rise divided by the number of bills with such higher prices. The significant average price rises with supplier codes are Rs.

3851 (Supplier 12), Rs. 2409.50 (28), Rs. 1692.50 (17), Rs. 1667.50 (27), Rs. 1605.50 (13), Rs. 1371.86 (05), Rs. 1244.85 (15), Rs. 1137.23 (03), Rs. 1099 (30) Rs. 1054 (08) and Rs. 1005.83 (19).

Table 4.1. Bills with Higher Prices for 2003-2004

Sl. No	Supplier Code	Bill No.	Initial Bill Value (Rs.)	Revised Bill Value (Rs.)	Savings to the Library (Rs.)
1	24	1428	2700	1963	737
2	24	1182	12561	10717	1844
3	28	1072	5545	5223	322
4	10	4	6763	6365	398
5	03	3613	4406	3887	519
6	03	3636	9537	9297	240
7	03	3612	14419	11766	2653
8	03	3635	11302	7168	4134
9	02	12	11128	10474	654
10	03	3615-A	31643	29533	2110
11	11	1	12800	12047	753
12	11	2	9598	9034	564
13	29	55	1053	995	58
14	29	56	2320	1933	387
15	29	54	8442	7504	938
16	08	301	9542	8488	1054
17	25	226	1514	1419	95
18	30	1073	20704	19605	1099
19	03	3677	4461	3567	894
20	03	3679	4808	4425	383
21	02	11	5611	5050	561
22	18	173	5919	5485	434
23	03	3670	4172	3948	224
24	04	86	6813	6412	401
25	29	71	2756	2584	172
26	17	108	744	700	44

Sl. No	Supplier Code	Bill No.	Initial Bill Value (Rs.)	Revised Bill Value (Rs.)	Savings to the Library (Rs.)
27	21	19 (B)	2923	2472	451
28	05	568	9037	8842	195
29	29	116	19324	17909	1415
30	29	119	3711	3488	223
31	17	104	1043	828	215
32	17	111	11923	9852	2071
33	17	105	13268	8828	4440
34	31	2146	1764	1660	104
35	27	978	31108	30181	927
36	13	3068	5052	2047	3005
37	07	13426	933	879	54
38	07	13425	806	711	95
39	02	41	11330	10742	588
40	19	3226	33712	33012	700
41	19	3227	5880	5530	350
42	31	2163	6270	5878	392
43	14	48	4310	3923	387
44	06	14891	1436	1364	72
45	03	3759	6304	3840	2464
46	16	119	6254	5203	1051
47	16	129	3777	3111	666
48	25	291	3735	1149	2586
49	19	2998	6560	2986	3574
50	05	612	3897	1947	1950
51	05	553	4639	3713	926
52	05	551	6506	3052	3454
53	05	555	4596	3181	1415
54	27	1015	2933	525	2408
55	16	120	3275	2707	568
56	10	36	2596	2077	519
57	01	4827	4477	4214	263

Sl. No	Supplier Code	Bill No.	Initial Bill Value (Rs.)	Revised Bill Value (Rs.)	Savings to the Library (Rs.)
58	32	2589	4876	4589	287
59	32	2590	3119	2740	379
60	32	2587	1520	1341	179
61	32	2586	1920	1694	226
62	13	3068	2047	1841	206
63	23	97	1842	1140	702
64	23	102	4381	3545	836
65	10	99	17956	16834	1122
66	20	16432	3854	3468	386
67	20	16433	8274	7927	347
68	24	146	7149	5918	1231
69	24	401	1004	941	63
70	24	398	1009	947	62
71	22	147D	2711	2552	159
72	10	107	18155	16275	1880
73	10	103	10603	9979	624
74	22	121B	6067	5455	612
75	16	121	3987	3296	691
76	10	109	4241	3855	386
77	01	4997	846	796	50
78	01	4979	506	476	30
79	01	4996	2156	2029	127
80	10	107	16275	15890	385
81	25	904	6155	5793	362
82	25	965	6818	6417	401
83	25	905	4810	4527	283
84	12	121	24754	20903	3851
85	05	567	4248	3356	892
86	05	604	4612	3841	771
87	18	756	9795	9218	577
88	28	1100	10213	7790	2423

Sl. No	Supplier Code	Bill No.	Initial Bill Value (Rs.)	Revised Bill Value (Rs.)	Savings to the Library (Rs.)
89	28	1102	5035	3737	1298
90	28	1098	7790	5712	2078
91	28	1107	5096	3691	1405
92	28	1104	10827	2791	8036
93	28	1092	6378	4501	1877
94	28	1080	10139	8302	1837
95	10	153	5774	5435	339
96	10	151	5774	4529	1245
97	19	3794	4273	3931	342
98	19	3795	14182	13674	508
99	03	4506-A	3805	3581	224
100	03	4605-A	3844	3618	226
101	03	4505	7499	7057	442
102	19	3819	9531	8970	561
103	03	4604-A	4615	4344	271
104	15	153	2879	2422	457
105	15	130	1971	1573	398
106	15	128	2285	2016	269
107	15	125	7270	6815	455
108	15	132	11869	9293	2576
109	15	124	4293	3730	563
110	15	129	7326	5520	1806
111	15	360	7238	5759	1479
112	15	206	9902	7724	2178
113	15	359	12164	8179	3985
114	15	361	4951	4060	891
115	15	362	2642	2331	311
116	15	363	5217	4402	815
					116602

Table 4.2 presents 77 bills of the financial year 2004-2005 where suppliers have quoted for prices higher than the

prevailing publisher prices at the time of supply leading to a saving of Rs. 67442 to the Library. Supplier 10 has 19 books with price quoted higher than what is marked by the publisher. Supplier 26 has 10 such cases and Supplier 01 with 7 such titles. Suppliers 03 and 29 have 5 titles quoting prices higher than the prevalent publisher prices. There is one supplier (11) with three cases, five suppliers (13, 18, 19, 38 and 41) with two cases, and six suppliers (09, 23, 37, 40, 42 and 43) have single cases of price overcharge. In a bill of Supplier 03, price overcharge of Rs. 5840 had been noticed. Suppliers with significant price increases over publisher prices are as follows: Supplier 19 (Rs. 3485), Supplier 26 (Rs. 3470), Supplier 29 (Rs. 3189), and Supplier 39 (Rs. 2846). If bills of price increases are considered together, five bills of Supplier 03 account for a saving of Rs. 11964 followed by nineteen bills of Supplier 10 resulting in a reduction of Rs. 9835 and ten bills of Supplier 26 leading to a benefit of Rs. 7893. Other cases worth highlighting are: Supplier 29 (five bills, Rs. 6255), Supplier 39 (six bills, Rs. 5524) and Supplier 15 (six bills, Rs. 5195). The average price rise for a supplier calculated as a measure of the total price rise divided by the number of bills with prices higher than the publishers' prices are Rs. 2932.80 (Supplier 03), Rs. 1927 (19), Rs. 1596 (41), Rs. 1251 (29), Rs. 920.67 (39), Rs. 865.83 (15) and Rs. 857 (13).

Table 4.2. Bills with Higher Prices for 2004-2005

Sl. No	Supplier Code	Bill No.	Initial Bill Value (Rs.)	Revised Bill Value (Rs.)	Savings to the Library (Rs.)
114	15	361	4951	4060	891
1	03	4879	3169	1585	1584
2	26	009	11451	10781	670
3	10	19	3010	2810	200
4	10	23	6559	6141	418
5	10	25	4514	4053	461

Sl. No	Supplier Code	Bill No.	Initial Bill Value (Rs.)	Revised Bill Value (Rs.)	Savings to the Library (Rs.)
6	10	20	6525	6091	434
7	10	22	18321	17100	1221
8	10	24	9585	8958	627
9	10	34	2930	2529	401
10	10	14	8556	8053	503
11	19	4311	6271	5902	369
12	26	89	250	188	62
13	26	87	6932	3462	3470
14	26	88	3667	3087	580
15	10	36	5728	5391	337
16	10	37	4066	3811	255
17	03	5081	8943	3103	5840
18	40	89	5762	5378	384
19	26	134	9178	8352	826
20	26	50	4722	4299	423
21	26	51	4722	4299	423
22	10	68	5309	4997	312
23	01	5628	14358	13907	451
24	15	134	5552	4698	854
25	23	39	12178	11414	764
26	37	284	4261	3637	624
27	26	51	4299	4046	253
28	10	29	5911	5772	139
29	10	36	4794	4217	577
30	01	5513	7225	6800	425
31	18	243	2916	2734	182
32	01	5724	21982	21158	824
33	18	276	7332	6753	579
34	13	6041	6470	5684	786
35	10	45	4435	4051	384
36	10	65	14894	13479	1415

Sl. No	Supplier Code	Bill No.	Initial Bill Value (Rs.)	Revised Bill Value (Rs.)	Savings to the Library (Rs.)
37	10	64	19543	19182	361
38	10	63	17918	17773	145
39	10	67	23950	22605	1345
40	10	66	24795	24495	300
41	43	1458	18261	17643	798
42	03	5987	17494	15450	2044
43	03	6045	3686	3317	369
44	03	6044	5753	3626	2127
45	01	5809	2380	1570	810
46	19	5284	8762	5277	3485
47	41	910	9707	8182	1525
48	41	1004	8705	7038	1667
49	11	580	5631	5300	331
50	11	583	23879	22810	1069
51	11	581	7518	6537	981
52	29	255	13078	12779	299
53	29	258	5446	5124	322
54	29	260	15148	11959	3189
55	29	262	6777	6379	398
56	39	368	18567	15721	2846
57	39	366	1411	1171	240
58	39	369	8635	8183	452
59	39	371	735	664	71
60	39	372	8814	7403	1411
61	39	365	8212	7708	504
62	15	1250	186	146	40
63	42	832	12441	11698	743
64	09	6614	6555	6063	492
65	26	10899	8292	7316	976
66	29	257	6110	4063	2047
67	26	421	4257	4047	210

Sl. No	Supplier Code	Bill No.	Initial Bill Value (Rs.)	Revised Bill Value (Rs.)	Savings to the Library (Rs.)
68	15	417	4481	3888	593
69	15	1356	15218	14235	983
70	15	1357	7581	5448	2133
71	15	1249	6178	5586	592
72	01	6382	4618	4346	272
73	38	241	6379	5980	399
74	38	251	6635	6064	571
75	01	6554	11603	11241	362
76	01	6683	15281	14326	955
77	13	3099	2708	1780	928
					67442

Table 4.3 presents 74 bills of the financial year 2005-2006 where suppliers have quoted for prices higher than the prevailing publisher prices at the time of supply leading to a saving of Rs. 85693 to the Library. Supplier18 has twenty five bills of price overshoot while supplier 15 has twenty two such cases. Supplier 26 has six bills charging prices higher than that announced by the publisher. Three suppliers (01, 12 and 29) have three similar cases each and another three suppliers (10, 23 ad 34) have two cases each. Six suppliers (02, 13, 16, 20, 21 and 35) have single cases of bills seeking prices higher than the publisher prices. In three bills of Supplier 26, price overcharges of Rs. 8974, Rs. 8257 and Rs. 6567 respectively had been noticed. Suppliers with significant price increases over publisher prices are as follows: Supplier 02 (Rs. 4500), Supplier 18 (Rs. 3910), Supplier 20 (Rs. 3660), Supplier 15 (two bills with Rs. 3612 and Rs. 3365), and Supplier 35 (Rs. 3173). While considering the price increases together, twenty five bills of Supplier 18 account for a saving of Rs. 25785 followed by six bills of Supplier 26 resulting in a reduction of Rs. 24968 and twenty

two bills of Supplier 15 leading to an advantage of Rs. 15346. The average price rise for a supplier calculated as a measure of the total price rise divided by the number of bills with prices higher than the publishers' prices are Rs. 4500 (Supplier 02), Rs. 4161.33 (26), Rs. 3660 (20), Rs. 3173 (35), Rs. 1031.40 (18), and Rs. 938.50 (23).

Table 4.3. Bills with Higher Prices for 2005-2006

Sl. No	Supplier Code	Bill No.	Initial Bill Value (Rs.)	Revised Bill Value (Rs.)	Savings to the Library (Rs.)
1	23	20	6991	5471	1520
2	29	127	9716	9124	592
3	29	130	3162	2961	201
4	29	120	6620	6305	315
5	26	543	6471	6090	381
6	26	444	17142	10575	6567
7	26	443	21730	13473	8257
8	02	42	4776	276	4500
9	01	5992	5812	5432	380
10	01	6536	3818	3568	250
11	12	108	16804	16518	286
12	12	109	4696	4403	293
13	12	103	6029	5732	297
14	10	122	3629	2927	702
15	10	121	2907	2725	182
16	34	104	7561	7089	472
17	21	13	1469	1256	213
18	16	211	2641	1961	680
19	15	327	3683	3508	175
20	23	48	5724	5367	357
21	15	439	6720	6581	139
22	15	348	6842	6265	577
23	15	241	3863	2863	1000
24	15	269	1696	1596	100

Sl. No	Supplier Code	Bill No.	Initial Bill Value (Rs.)	Revised Bill Value (Rs.)	Savings to the Library (Rs.)
25	15	172	4697	4372	325
26	26	605	10064	9472	592
27	26	588	3355	3158	197
28	34	105	5258	4929	329
29	15	570	35162	32964	2198
30	15	430	57788	54176	3612
31	15	099	6709	6334	375
32	15	272	5461	4959	502
33	15	603	4946	4655	291
34	13	7008	15207	14566	641
35	15	316	10684	7319	3365
36	15	1228	10546	10155	391
37	15	329	1042	1003	39
38	15	203	5797	5730	67
39	15	118	4103	3647	456
40	15	455	1302	1115	187
41	15	334	1411	1301	110
42	26	627	29251	20277	8974
43	01	762	8612	8061	551
44	15	644	7589	6823	766
45	15	298	7589	7391	198
46	15	586	15185	14931	254
47	18	1521	2459	2333	126
48	18	1525	10673	9412	1261
49	18	1558	3425	3290	135
50	18	1556	5989	5508	481
51	18	1534	10975	9109	1866
52	18	1557	5852	5382	470
53	20	16602	112227	108567	3660
54	15	740	3727	3508	219
55	18	1100	1588	1461	127

Sl. No	Supplier Code	Bill No.	Initial Bill Value (Rs.)	Revised Bill Value (Rs.)	Savings to the Library (Rs.)
56	18	1085	10155	7327	2828
57	18	1090	22381	20283	2098
58	18	1080	22466	18556	3910
59	18	1104	6272	3492	2780
60	35	29	6446	3273	3173
61	18	1086	5122	4024	1098
62	18	1088	12766	11669	1097
63	18	1534	10975	10329	646
64	18	1075	2542	1525	1017
65	18	1273	4647	3716	931
66	18	1283	3082	2767	315
67	18	1296	4495	2885	1610
68	18	1295	2138	1853	285
69	18	1284	15284	14912	372
70	18	1296	4495	4092	403
71	18	1297	1572	1447	125
72	18	1276	3631	3260	371
73	18	1111	11200	10480	720
74	18	1278	3566	2853	713
					85693

6. SUPPLIER QUOTING LESSER PRICES

It was also found that there were cases in which the supplier quoted prices less than the current publisher prices. Since the checking was done with the prices quoted on the website, the prices may be changed in between the supplier preparing/submitting the bill and its formal verification by the Library. There may also be cases where the supplier might have obtained the book from the importer/distributor at a lesser price. Specific cases for two financial years 2003-2004 and 2004-2005 are highlighted below. Table 5.3

highlights the exchange rates used for assessing the rupee value for foreign currencies Pound, Dollar and Euro to calculate the savings accrued from this category of price reduction.

Table 5.1 summarizes 105 cases for the financial year 2003-2004 where the supplier offered books to the library at prices lower than the prevailing publisher prices. These cases lead to a saving of Rs. 117,180 to the Library. One book of Supplier 03 could achieve a saving of Rs. 13760. Other cases worth mentioning substantial difference in prices are: Rs. 5975.80 (Supplier 22), Rs. 5129.05 (04), Rs. 4135.50 (30), Rs. 3216.50 (15), Rs. 2969.45 (34), Rs. 2759.30 (28), Rs. 2527.25 (15) and Rs. 2511.63 (18). There are four cases where the publisher price is higher than the offered price by Rs. 2000-2500, twenty two books where the price offered is less than the publisher price by Rs. 1000-2000, thirty cases in which the price difference is in between Rs. 500-1000 and forty one cases with price difference less than Rs. 500. Supplier 15 supplied 25 titles totaling Rs. 26341 lower than the publisher prices added together. Twelve titles were offered by Supplier 03 at Rs. 21917 lesser than the prevalent publisher prices. Supplier 22 delivered nine titles at prices lower from publisher's rates by Rs. 9112. Other significant cases include Supplier 18 (5651.13), Supplier 04 (Rs. 5587.97), Supplier 28 (Rs. 5469.79), Supplier 01 (Rs. 5448.05) and Suplier 23 (Rs. 5087.21). In the case of average price difference, one book of Supplier 30 carried a difference of Rs. 4135.40, one book of Supplier 34 yielded a profit of Rs. 2969.45, and books offered by Supplier 04 lead to a price benefit of Rs. 2793.99. Supplier 29 (Rs. 1889.65), 03 (Rs. 1826.43), 28 (Rs. 1823.26), 35 (Rs. 1378.50), 19 (Rs. 1131.09), 25 (Rs. 1125.77), 24 (Rs. 1079.80), 09 (Rs. 1063.75), 05 (Rs. 1055.30), 15 (Rs. 1053.63) and 22 (Rs. 1012.50) are incidences of books supplied to Library at average prices lesser than publisher prices by Rs. 1000-2000. There are five cases where this difference varies from Rs. 500 to Rs. 950 and four cases where the difference is less than Rs. 500.

Table 5.1. Bills with Higher Publisher Prices for 2003-2004

Sl. No	Supplier Code	Bill No.	Initial Bill Value (Rs.)	Revised Bill Value (Rs.)	Savings to the Library (Rs.)
1	25	587	$129.95	$89.95	$40
2	22	83	$39.95	$27.95	$12
3	25	667	€104.95	€84.95	€20
4	29	104	€104.95	€69.95	€35
5	21	19(C)	$29.95	$26.95	$3
6	22	47A	$725	$594.95	$130.05
7	09	6096	$150	$97.5	$52.5
8	35	26	$285	$235	$30
9	18	293	$180	$151.95	$28.05
10	03	3759	$52.95	$47.95	$5
11	19	3229	€149.95	€129	€20.95
12	03	3795	$55	$47.5	$7.5
13	03		$59.95	$18	$41.95
14	03	3796	£275	£98	£177
15	03		£69.99	£40	£29.99
	03		$79.95	$75	$4.95
16	03	3797	$149.95	$120	$29.95
17	04	258	€93.5	€85	€8.5
18	03	3759	$52.95	$47.95	$5
19	03		$69	$50	$19
20	24	296	€144.95	€124.95	€20
21	18	243	$92.66	$38	$54.66
22	05	550	€89.95	€79.95	€10
23	05		€109.95	€99.95	€10
24	30	1103	$690	$600	$90
25	10	35	$135	$119	$16
26	22	147B	$95	$85	$10
27	22		$55	$45	$10

Sl. No	Supplier Code	Bill No.	Initial Bill Value (Rs.)	Revised Bill Value (Rs.)	Savings to the Library (Rs.)
28	22	46H	$95	$87.95	$7.05
29	18	111	$94.5	$89.95	$4.55
30	18	291	€119.95	€99.95	€20
31	18	292	€129	€122	€7
32	22	132B	$101	$98	$3
33	33	143	$85.5	$84	$1.5
34	33	141	$74	$66.67	$7.33
35	15	364	$83.95	$51	$32.95
36	15	153	€62.95	€52.95	€10
37	28	1094	$94.95	$79.95	$15
38	18	110	$83.95	$79.95	$4
39	09	6100	$70	$59.95	$10.05
40	09	310	$105	$79.95	$25.05
41	15	365	$115	$109.95	$5.05
42	11	57	$132	$125	$7
43	22	85	£45	£39.99	£5.01
44	14	80	€104.95	€94.95	€10
45	14		$88.95	$79.95	$9
46	01	4752	£55	£45	£10
47	01	4758	£95	£82.5	£12.5
48	15	129	$86.95	$59.95	$27
49	15	363	$139.95	$125.96	$14
50	15	132	$140	$105	$35
51	15		$155	$119.95	$35.05
52	15	360	£75	£49.95	£25.05
53	15	206	$265	$195	$70
54	15	359	£105	£95	£10
55	15	128	£60	£52	£8
56	15		€99.95	€89.95	€10
57	15		$189.95	$179.95	$10
58	23	49	$115	$95	$20

Sl. No	Supplier Code	Bill No.	Initial Bill Value (Rs.)	Revised Bill Value (Rs.)	Savings to the Library (Rs.)
59	15	134	$149.95	$99.95	$50
60	23	47	$105	$89.95	$15.05
61	23	147	$105	$99.95	$5.05
62	23	48	€69.95	€49.95	€20
63	23	43	$67.95	$59.95	$8
64	23	120	$99.95	$84.95	$15
65	23	99	$89.95	$77	$12.95
66	23	103	€104.5	€95	€9.5
67	15	500	£85	£75	£10
68	04	510	€155	€60	€95
69	09		$89.95	$84.95	$5
70	32	2585	$103	$86	$17
71	32	2591	$118	$98	$20
72	32	2581	$46	$38	$8
73	34	1302	€199.95	€144.95	€55
74	10	105	$84.95	$79.95	$5
75	01	4593	€104.95	€94.95	€10
76	22	147E	$53	$49.95	$3.05
77	22	182B	€139.5	€127	€12.5
78	10	109	$110	$100	$10
79	33	238	$94	$78	$16
80	01	5081	£30	1650	750
81	01	4979A	£24.99	1350	649
82	01	4996A	£20	1100	500
83	01	4996B	445	395	50
84	01		£40	1990	1210
85	25	600	$189.95	$179.95	$10
86	05	567	€109.95	€79	€30.95
87	05	604	$130	$98	$32
88	33	143	€105	€98.95	€6.05
89	33	319	$93.5	$89.95	$3.55

Sl. No	Supplier Code	Bill No.	Initial Bill Value (Rs.)	Revised Bill Value (Rs.)	Savings to the Library (Rs.)
90	33	142	€144.5	€115	€29.5
91	15	779	\$250	\$195	\$55
92	15	888	\$160	\$150	\$10
93	15	881	£28	1495	745
94	15	780	\$139	\$99	\$40
95	15	883	£85	£79.5	£5.5
96	15	882	£29.95	£24.95	£5
97	15	887	\$119.95	\$109.95	\$10
98	28	1102	£85	£59	£26
99	28	1092	\$180	\$119.95	\$60.05
100	15	928	£160	£150	£10
101	15	929	\$105	\$99.95	\$5.05
102	03	4606	£24.99	£22.99	£2
103	03	4605A	\$105	\$99.95	\$5.05
104	03	4604A	\$125	\$120	\$5
105	15	946	\$69.95	\$59.95	\$10
		\$ 1367.99 X Rs. 45.95 = Rs. 62859.14 +€ 449.95 X Rs. 53.99 = Rs. 24292.80 +£ 336.05 X Rs. 77.74 = Rs. 26124.53 +Rs. 3904Total: Rs. 1,17,180.47			

Table 5.2 highlights 92 cases where the supplier has charged prices below the prevalent publisher prices leading to a saving of Rs. 81561 to the Library. Supplier 03 supplied a book to the library at a price Rs. 9215 lower than the publisher's latest price and Supplier 20 did the same for another book at a price lower by Rs. 7192. Similarly Supplier 37 delivered a book at a price Rs. 6221 lower than the publisher price and Supplier 18 could supply a book at a price Rs. 4147.50 below the publisher's price at that instant. Supplier 03 provided a book for Rs. 3144 lesser than the publisher price. There are five cases (three from Supplier 15 and one each from Suppliers 40 and 10) where books are

offered to the library at prices in the range of Rs. 2000-3000 lower than the prices announced by the respective publisher. There are seven cases where the price difference is in between Rs. 1000-2000, twenty cases in between Rs. 500-1000 and fifty five cases where the difference between publisher price and offered price is less than Rs. 500. Supplier 15 supplied 16 books at prices lower than the publisher prices together accounting for Rs. 14366 and Supplier 03 did the same for four books resulting in a saving of Rs. 13685. Fourteen books were offered by Supplier 18 at prices lesser than the publisher prices by Rs. 9387. Other cases resulting in major gains are Supplier 37 (5 books, Rs. 9140), Supplier 20 (3 books, Rs. 7596.55) and Supplier 01 (13 books, Rs. 5850). Average price reduction calculated for a supplier as a measure of the total price difference offered by the supplier divided by the number of books supplied gives the following results: Supplier 03 (Rs. 3421), Supplier 20 (Rs. 2532), Supplier 40 (Rs. 2247.50), Supplier 37 (Rs. 1828) and Supplier 06 (1412). There are three suppliers (15, 10, and 18) with differences in between Rs. 500 and Rs. 1000 and eight suppliers for which the difference is less than Rs. 500.

Table 5.2. Bills with Higher Publisher Prices for 2004-2005

Sl. No	Supplier	Bill No.	Publisher Price	Offered Price	Savings to the Library
1	07	203301	$115.95	$99.95	$16
2	07	203301	$105	$94.95	$10.05
3	07	203301	$95	$89.95	$5.05
4	06	15523	€148.95	€119	€29.95
5	06	15521	€84.95	€64.95	€20
6	15	68	$63.50X2	$59.95X2	$7.10
7	01	5314	£65	£62	£3
8	01	5340	1834	1250	584
9	36	223	€84.95	€64,95	€20
10	36	222	$148	$135	$13
11	15	116	2933	1950	983

Sl. No	Supplier	Bill No.	Publisher Price	Offered Price	Savings to the Library
12	15	140	£110	£80	£30
13	36	245	€64.15	€59.95	€4.2
14	36	243	€53.45	€49.95	€3.5
15	36	243	€128.35	€119.95	€8.4
16	36	242	€106.95	€99.95	€7
17	19	4259	€181.95	€169.85	€11.9
18	19	4261	€106.95	€99.95	€7
19	10	20	$117	$105	$12
20	10	20	$94.95	$89.95	$5
21	37	303	£40	£35	£5
22	37	385	$179.5	$150	$29.5
23	37	385	€275	€165	€110
24	15	129	$28	$24.95	$3.05
25	10	20	$94.95	$89.95	$5
26	40	90	$165	$115	$50
27	20	16669	$83.95	$79.95	$4
28	03	5291	$1055	$850	$205
29	03	5231	£48.99	£34.99	£14
30	10	56	£32.95	£27.50	£5.45
31	18	264	£475	£425	£50
32	01	5546	€229	€199	€30
33	15	368	5400	2690	2710
34	15	368	1348	895	453
35	10	67	€79.95	€42.95	€37
36	34	182	€136.96	€128	€8.96
37	34	180	$94.95	$89.95	$5
38	37	284	£70	£65	£5
39	37	470	$157	$140	$17
40	01	5756	€149.75	€139.95	€9.80
41	01	5673	$34	$31.50	$2.50
42	01	5534	€79.95	€69.95	€10
43	01	5535	$141.75	$135	$6.75

Sl. No	Supplier	Bill No.	Publisher Price	Offered Price	Savings to the Library
44	15	591	$131	$115	$16
45	15	616	$186	$135	$51
46	18	5724	$210	$197.95	$12.05
47	13	6040	€111.28	€104	€7.28
48	13	6040	€115.56	€108	€7.56
49	19	4565	£29.95	£24.95	£5
50	19	4566	£22.95	£19.95	£3
51	19	4566	£32.95	£29.95	£3
52	18	506	€130.54	€122	€8.54
53	34	320	€53.45	€49.95	€4
54	18	375	£67.95	£64.50	£3.45
55	26	186	£134	£128	£6
56	34	278	£35	£24	£11
57	18	514	$60	$49.95	$10.05
58	34	334	$140	$132	$8
59	15	654	€85.55	€79.95	€5.60
60	18	393	€158.36	€148	€10.36
61	18	391	€64.15	€59.95	€4.20
62	18	388	€74.85	€69.95	€4.90
63	20	16599	$455	$295	$160
64	20	16600	$129.95	$124.95	$5
65	01	5226	824	395	429
66	03	4910	$1469.95	$1400	$69.95
67	07	87	$57.95	$49.95	$8
68	03	4864	£26.99	£25	£1.99
69	01	5271	€104.95	€99.95	€5
70	15	17	€64.95	€49.95	€15
71	18	28	$150	$140	$10
72	18	31	$575	$550	$25
73	18	29	$59.95	$57.50	$2.45
74	01	5079	£36.99	£35	£1.99
75	34	44	€68	€63.55	€4.45

Sl. No	Supplier	Bill No.	Publisher Price	Offered Price	Savings to the Library
76	36	187	$76	$66.67	$9.33
77	15	13	$130	$120	$10
78	01	5274	719	395	324
79	32	02714	$74	$62	$12
80	32	02714	$34	$28	$6
81	32	02714	$82	$68	$14
82	32	02714	$65	$54	$11
83	01	5263	$43.95	$39.95	$4
84	01	5296	$74	$65	$9
85	15	331	£91	£82	£9
86	18	390	€96.25	€89.95	€6.30
87	18	385	€37.40	€34.95	€2.45
88	18	385	€53.50	€50	€3.50
89	15	842	€114.49	€107	€7.49
90	15	842	€159.97	€149.50	€10.47
91	15	834	€161.57	€151	€10.57
92	15	835	€78.11	€73	€5.11

$ 848.83 X Rs. 44.95 = Rs. 38154.91
+€ 440.49 X Rs. 56.55 = Rs. 24909.71
+£ 156.88 X Rs. 82.95 = Rs. 13013.20
+Rs. 5483Total: Rs. 81560.82

Table 5.3. Exchange rates used

Sl. No	Average RBI Exchange Rate	2003-2004	2004-2005
1	US $	45.95	44.95
2	Euro €	53.99	56.55
3	UK £	77.74	82.95

7. SAVINGS TO THE LIBRARY THROUGH PRICE VERIFICATION

Table 6 below shows the overall savings to the Library as a result of strictly adhering to verifying the best possible and correctly available prices for books supplied to the library through two categories of supplier quoting prices higher than and lower than the prevailing prices available from publishers' sources. The library could achieve over Rs. 2.34 lakhs (4% of total expenditure for buying books; 10 lakhs = 1million) saving in the financial year 2003-2004 whereas this fell to Rs. 1.49 lakhs (2.14%) in the next financial year. In the financial year 2005-2006, due to difficulties in cumulating the data for supplier prices lower than publisher prices, only the first category of saving, Rs. 85693 (1.48%) is considered. Though no exhaustiveness is claimed in the data presented considering the difficulties mentioned earlier, one reason for the falling percentages could be that the suppliers noticed the strictness adopted by the library in verifying the prices quoted and hence were more accurate in furnishing bills and price proofs. The actual savings generated from stricter price verification is much beyond the figures mentioned because the rigorous checking resorted by the library might have discouraged suppliers from further bringing exploded bills with problematic prices to library. Stricter price certification would definitely act as a deterrent and lead to optimum utilization of budget available for purchasing books by ensuring that every rupee spent is genuinely done.

Table 6. Savings to the Library through Price Verification

Sl. No	Financial Year	Savings with Publ. Price (Sup. quoting higher price)	Savings from Offered Price (Supplier quoting lower price)	Savings to the Library	% of the Total Annual Expenditure
1	2003-2004	Rs. 116602	Rs. 117180.47	Rs. 233782.47	4.12
2	2004-2005	Rs. 67442	Rs. 81560.82	Rs. 149002.82	2.14
3	2005-2006	Rs. 85693		Rs. 85693	1.48

8. CHALLENGES AND OPPORTUNITIES

A professional acquisition system must strive at the same time to optimize the speed of different operations and ensure that the different stakeholders involved should adhere to a standard set of practices in dealing with it. The interesting results gathered by a major acquisition system in the country with respect to going an extra inch in ensuring that the documents submitted by trade parties to the library are genuine and exploring the virtues of information technology and web in conducting the different operations. While adopting these measures, some of the suppliers hitherto not experienced with such an inspection from the Library raised certain objections and hue and cry. But slowly they realized that the rules and regulations put in place are unbiased and give a level playing field to all the parties involved, thus the library received constructive support and active cooperation from each and every supplier.

Libraries shall adopt a strategy that the publisher is the only agency who can dictate the correct price of a book and higher price charged by any other agency (importer/ distributor/supplier) should be treated as null and void while dealing with price verification. Any other concocted document furnished to charge higher prices must be discarded forthwith and put suppliers conducting such practices on the watch list and those continuing to do so over a period of time should be blacklisted. Taking such measures against few such suppliers would signal the warning to others too.

Sometimes the supplier used to bring import documents suggesting that the prices quoted by the publisher's site are not available to the country. Nowadays, this fact can be easily ascertained as many of the premier international publishers have made country specific websites revealing the correct prices applicable to a particular country. If this sort of verification is not possible from the web site, the library should get proper document from the publisher before sanctioning such import prices which are often higher than the publisher's prices.

Suppliers are of various types with respect to their turn over, number of clients, overheads involved etc. Some suppliers give preference to earlier processing of bills and they normally comply with the problems pointed out by the library and submit fresh bills accordingly. Some other suppliers delay to comply with inconsistencies regarding price and discount pointed out and this may lead to delayed processing of books. So library should evolve an action plan and prescribe specific time period for suppliers to submit revised bills/collecting back the books concerned when errors are pointed out by library to avoid such delays.

Healthy library supplier relationship would only hold well in a transparent system. Library professionals should adopt an unbiased approach towards their suppliers and suppliers should serve their client libraries without any preference or ill will. With acquisition systems in libraries getting transformed as collection development and access management systems, suppliers and library professionals being equal takers in providing information support to users should hence reassess their roles and learn from each others experiences to perform well in their respective domains.

A supplier concerned only at earning the maximum profit from a library for each and every book supplied is not in tune with the times where business consolidation, market focus and positioning are emerging as effective strategies for doing better business. Libraries should keep a watch on those suppliers who are not respecting the acquisition goals of the institution.

Disciplines like management and computer science attracts lot of reprints or local editions of front ranking titles. With developed countries accepting India as a major BPO destination, education and human resources development in the country has transcended the national borders and hence considerable number of text books in different disciplines are also getting reprinted liberally either through branch offices of the international publishers or through business associates or rights transfer to local publishers. But still there is a long wait for any such arrangement for research level books which drain the country's resources tremendously.

With Xeroxing, scanning and other duplicating techniques producing copies as good as the original, suppliers can easily furnish proofs required by libraries. Since they also have good business relationships with many distributors/importers/sellers, the library professionals have a tough time in ascertaining what is genuine and what is not. Perhaps opening of better communication channels and close linkages of professionals working in acquisition units in different institutions would help to effectively deal with doubtful trade practices, special prices from publishers, problematic suppliers, fake documents so that collectively we can learn more in less time.

Libraries cite time as one of the reasons for accepting whatever documents provided by the supplier. Our experience shows that price verification attempted here has not taken more time or delayed acquisition work in any way. In professional work, convincing ourselves is the first step to ensure that the operations are conducted in a healthy manner.

9. CONCLUSION

Till publishers marking copy numbers in books and purchase invoices to avoid any exploitation of one invoice for multiple deals by distributors/sellers/suppliers, libraries have to evolve special procedures to ascertain the correct prices charged by suppliers for books procured. Being a professional activity, the emerging technological options could be used to efficiently perform the various operations in an acquisition system. This showed how the relevant information available in web sites of publishers might be used to verify the price proof offered by book suppliers. The results for three financial years based on specific cases where the suppliers quoted more price than the publisher price and cases where the suppliers charged lesser reveal interesting results about the utility of such measures for further strengthening of the acquisition operations. Suppliers 02, 04, 06, 08, 09, 12, 14, 16, 30, 35, 37 supplied less number of titles at prices higher than the publishers prices compared to other suppliers. Suppliers 15, 03, 18, 37, 20, 01, 22, 04 and 28 brought more books at prices less than the publishers' prices compared to others. This exercise helped the acquisition staff to identify the nuances of the multiplicity of documents furnished by various suppliers and ascertaining the most authentic ones. Enforcing a tough validation procedure for certifying the prices of books purchased shall discourage problematic suppliers from tampering with the system and save the library from continuing to do business with problematic suppliers. The results gathered could also be extended for vendor rating though it is not attempted at this stage.

REFERENCES

1. Hewitt, Joe A. On the nature of acquisitions, Library Resources & Technical Services, 33 (2); pp. 105-122.
2. ALA,http://www.ala.org/Template.cfm?Section=Collection_Development&template=/ContentManagement/ContentDisplay.cfm&ContentID=26942
3. Cogswell, J, The organization of collection management functions in academic research libraries, Journal of Academic Librarianship, 13, 1987, pp. 268-276.
4. Basu, A. K., Ghosh, K. K., Impact of price hike and soring foreign exchange conversion rates on special libraries, Annals of Library Science and Documentation, 24 (2) June 77, pp. 86-91.

5. Guha, A. K., Buha, B., Jayaswal, P. K., Book prices and their impact on libraries, ILA Bulletin, 16 (1-2) Jan June 80, pp. 50-62.

6. Sharma, Narinder Kumar, The impact of rising prices of books on the development of libraries, ILA Bulletin, 16 (1-2) Jan June 80, pp. 81-85.

7. Satyanarayana, D., Satyanarayana, I., Economic constraints and effective collection development in university libraries in India, Proceedings of the 19th All India Conference of IASLIC, Calcutta, India, 26-29 December 1993, pp. 67-71.

8. Bhatt, R. K., Book acquisition programme in libraries and information centres under the financial crunch, Herald of Library Science, 34 (1-2) Jan-Apr 95, pp. 20-26.

9. Reddy, Y. N.; Suseela, V. J., Periodical prices in relation to mailing charges, foreign exchange and inflation, IASLIC Bulletin, 40 (3) Sep 95, pp. 107-116.

10. Ismail, Mohamed, Library collections and the effect of rising prices of books in India, Herald of Library Science, 27 (3-4) July-Oct 88, pp. 177-180.

11. Clifford, Peter. Fixing a price, Bookseller, (5146) 17 Sep 2004, pp. 24-26.

12. Sylge, C., One world, one book price?, Bookseller, (4867) 9 Apr 1999, pp. 22-25.

13. Duchin, Douglas, The apparently automatic self-inflating price of books, Library Acquisitions: Practice and Theory, 13 (2) 1989, pp. 115-118.

14. Philipson, Morris, Intrinsic value versus market value, Library Quarterly, 54 (1) Jan 84, pp. 13-20.

6

RESEARCH COLLABORATION

1. INTRODUCTION

The recent spurt in publication activity reveals some interesting aspects, especially after the widespread availability of internet in libraries and cyber cafes. There is no doubt that the Internet has become a great leveler in the flow of information that now professionals from smaller institutions also have access to a wide range of information resources. Another fact that has contributed to the rising number of publications is demand and supply. On the one hand there is a demand for professionals to be active and academic minded evidenced through publications for better professional prospects and on the other hand there is also a demand for more papers in the professional domain warranted by the increasing number of new conferences, wider participation and interest in existing annual conferences, festschrift volumes, editorial works and even authored books. With computer and information technology becoming an area of key focus in the discipline, like the wide ranging publications erupted in superconductivity or materials science, professionals can publish papers on conceptual, evaluative or implementation themes on an array of topics. There are also collaborative publications with the same set of authors' writing papers on similar topics in same or different publications. The primary focus of this paper is to identify the extent of such collaboration among some of the recent publications in the field of library and information science.

2. METHODOLOGY

To assess the partnership in professional publications two successive years of publication pattern in proceedings of conferences of CALIBER, the annual conference organized by INFLIBNET Centre [1,2], Indian Library Association [3, 4] and Society for Information Science [5, 6] and two consecutive volumes of journals, volume 22, issues 1-6 for 2002 and volume 23, issues 1-6 for 2003 of DESIDOC Bulletin of Information Technology [7, 8] and volume 47, issues 1-4 for 2002 and volume 48, issues 1-4 for 2003 of IASLIC Bulletin [9, 10] are analyzed in this study. All the conferences and journals covered in the study review papers before publishing them and hence vouch for the scholarly nature of research published in them. For the sake of clarity in analysis, library professionals are classified in three categories of, working library professionals (designated as Librarian in the study with abbreviation P), teachers of library and information science (designated as Teacher in the study with abbreviation T), and students, apprentices, trainees and others working in temporary projects (designated as Student in the study with abbreviation S). The concerned proceedings volumes and journal issues were browsed to collect data in the following manner:

- Number of articles by single authors and identifying the author is a Librarian/Teacher/ Student
- Number of articles by two authors, three authors and those with four or more than four authors
- In the case of articles by multiple authors, first author

is a Librarian/Teacher/ Student, second author is a Librarian/Teacher/ Student, and other author(s) is/are Librarian/Teacher/ Student

- In the case of articles by multiple authors, the authors are from the same institution or not.
- In the case of articles by multiple authors, if the authors are from different institutions, the institutions are in the same place or in different places.

2.1. Limitations of the Study

Data for successive years of the publications covered and some other journals such as Annals (NISCAIR) Journal of Information Management (SRELS), and Herald of Library Science could not be included in the study due to lack of immediate availability of the concerned journal issues. Other than collaboration, the discussion has purposely excluded other aspects like authors, subject matter, affiliation, citations etc., because the basic objective here is to identify publishing trends of three categories of professionals: teachers, librarians and students.

3. DATAANALYSIS

Publication trends in terms of the total number of papers and papers by single author and multiple authors with percentages in each category to the respective totals are tabulated in Table 1. The study covers a total of 627 papers. Out of the journals and conference volumes studied, a large number of papers are in the proceedings volume of SIS 2004 (99) followed by SIS 2003 (95), ILA 2003 (94) and CALIBER 2004 (79). In the case of journals, IALSIC Bulletin for 2002 has 20 papers followed by the same for 2003 with 19 papers and DBIT 2003 with an equal number of articles. Only 44% of the overall number of articles is by single authors though the largest number of collaborated papers (38% two-author papers) is still lower than the single author papers. The number of papers falls down steeply when the number of authors increases. Only 24 out of 627 papers are through partnerships involving more than four authors and the number of three author papers is approximately one third of the two-author papers.

In the case of CALIBER 2003, majority of the papers are by single authors (46%) followed by papers with two authors (36%) and there are 4 four author papers. Along with 67 papers in full text, the volume also contained 38 abstracts of which again the maximum (over 63%) are by single authors. In the conference volume of CALIBER 2004, maximum number of the total of 79 papers are by two author partnership (over 49%) followed by single author (30%) and 3 author partnership (16%). Eight of the 14 abstracts included in the Proceedings are out of two-author partnership, around 29% by single author, and 14% by three author collaboration. Out of the 15 papers in DBIT 2002, majority are by two-author partnership (6, 40%), four are by single authors, two each are out of three-author collaboration and four-author collaborations, and one paper written jointly by five authors. Eight papers each in DBIT 2003 are by single authors and through two-author collaborations, and three papers are produced by partnerships involving three authors. In contrast to DBIT, large number of single authored papers is published in IASLIC Bulletin; 50% of papers in 2002 and 63% of papers in 2003 in the IASLIC Bulleting are by single authors followed by papers of two and three author partnerships. One paper in 2002 and two papers in 2003 are written by four-author collaboration. In the case of ILA conferences, majority of papers are produced by single authors (49% in 2003 and 44% in 2004). 35% of papers in 2003 and 41% in 2004 in the proceedings volume of ILA are through two-author partnerships. Three papers in ILA 2004 involve four author collaborations. 51% of papers in SIS 2003 are produced by single authors whereas 48% of papers in SIS 2004 are by two-author partnership.

Table 1. Publication Trends in Journals and Proceedings of Conferences

Conference/ Journal	Single author #	% of Total	2 authors #	% of Total	3 authors #	% of Total	>=4 authors #	% of Total	Total Papers
CALIBER 2003	31	46.27	24	35.62	8	11.94	4	5.97	67
CALIBER Abstracts	24	63.16	9	23.68	4	10.53	1	2.63	38
CALIBER 2004	27	30.38	39	49.37	13	16.46			79
CALIBER Abstracts	4	28.57	8	57.14	2	14.28			14
DBIT 2002	4	26.67	6	40.00	2	13.33	3	20.00	15
DBIT 2003	8	42.11	8	42.11	3	15.79			19
IASLIC B 2002	10	50.00	6	30.00	3	15.00	1	5.00	20
IASLIC B 2003	12	63.16	3	15.79	2	10.53	2	10.53	19
ILA 2003	46	48.54	33	35.11	12	12.76	3	3.19	94
ILA 2004	30	44.12	28	41.18	10	14.71			68
SIS 2003	49	51.58	30	31.58	15	15.79	1	1.05	95
SIS 2004	31	31.31	48	48.48	11	11.11	9	9.09	99
Total	276	44.02	242	38.59	85	13.56	24	3.83	627

Single author papers are categorized as per the nature of job of the author in Table 2. Over 63% of the 276 single author papers are authored by librarians, 25% by teachers, and 8% by students whereas designation of the author is not clear with 12 papers. Other than DBIT, which has 50% each of the authors are Librarians or Teachers, in all other journals and conference volumes studied, professional librarians have an edge over teachers and students in the number of papers published. Out of the 276 single authored papers, 63% are by working library professionals, around 25% by Teachers of LIS, about 8% by students, and designation is not clear in the case 12 papers (4%). Out of 31 single author papers in CALIBER 2003, 19 (61%) are by librarians, 10 (32%) are by teachers, and 2 (6%) are by students and 62% of the single author abstracts in this volume are by librarians. The number of papers by librarians, teachers and students in the CALIBER 2004 volume are respectively 18 (67%), 5 (18%) and 4 (15%) and 3 of the four single author abstracts are written by librarians. Two each of the four single author papers in DBIT 2002 and four each of the eight single author papers in DBIT 2003 are authored by librarians and teachers. In the case of ten single author papers in IASLIC Bulletin 2002, seven are produced by librarians, two by teachers and designation is not clear in the case of one paper, as it is a habit in the case of many library professionals working in junior level and research scholars and students of LIS to just give only their Institution name while publishing papers. There are twelve single author papers in IASLIC Bulletin 2003 of which six are by librarians, five by teachers and one by student. Out of the 46 single author papers in ILA 2003, twenty eight (61%) are authored by librarians, ten (22%) are by teachers, four (9%) by students and designation of the author is not obvious in the case of the remaining four papers. Half of the thirty single author papers in ILA 2004 are produced by librarians, followed by nine (30%) by teachers, one by student, and designation is not provided for the remaining five papers. Librarians have to their credit thirty four (69%) of the 49 single author papers in SIS 2003 whereas twelve papers were written by teachers and the remaining three had students as authors. In the case of SIS 2004, twenty three single author papers (74%) are authored by librarians while 16% by teachers, one paper by a student and the designation not marked in the case of two papers.

Analysis of papers with more than one author is highlighted with features of the first, second, and other authors in Tables 3-5. As in the case of single author papers, librarians are active as first author in maximum number of collaborated papers (over 63% of collaborated papers have librarian as first author in contrast to 27% of such papers with teachers as first author). About 8% of the collaborated papers have students as the first author and designation of authors is not clear in the case of six many-authored papers.

Table 2. Single Author Papers

Conference/ Journal	Single Author								
	Librarian (P)		Teacher (T)		Student (S)		No Designation		Total
	#	%	#	%	#	%	#	%	
CALIBER 2003	19	61.29	10	32.26	2	6.45			31
CALIBER Abstracts	15	62.50	4	16.67	5	20.83			24
CALIBER 2004	18	66.67	5	18.52	4	14.81			27
CALIBER Abstracts	3	75.00			1	25.00			4
DBIT 2002	2	50.00	2	50.00					4
DBIT 2003	4	50.00	4	50.00					8
IASLIC B 2002	7	70.00	2	20.00			1	10.00	10
IASLIC B 2003	6	50.00	5	41.67	1	8.33			12
ILA 2003	28	60.87	10	21.74	4	8.69	4	8.69	46
ILA 2004	15	50.00	9	30.00	1	3.33	5	16.67	30
SIS 2003	34	69.38	12	24.49	3	6.12			49
SIS 2004	23	74.19	5	16.13	1	3.23	2	6.45	31
Total	174	63.04	68	24.64	22	7.97	12	4.35	276

In the case of CALIBER 2003, out of the thirty six papers having more than one author, 24 (67%) are by librarians as the first author, nine such papers have teachers as the first author and in the case of 3 papers, students had the privilege to be the first author. Out of the fourteen abstracts of multiple authors, half had librarians as the first author, five such abstracts are authored by a group of authors with a teacher of LIS as the first author, and two abstracts had student as the first author. Of the 52 papers with multiple authors in CALIBER 2004, 32 had librarians as the first author, 16 with teachers as the first author and for four papers, the first author happens to be a student. Out of the 10 abstracts printed in this volume, seven had librarian as the first author, two had teacher as the first author and one with student as the first author. For DBIT 2002, 10 of 11 papers are by multiple authors lead by a librarian as the first author and one paper has a teacher as the first author. In the case of DBIT 2003, eight out of eleven multi authored papers had librarians as the first author, one paper with teacher as the first author and two papers with students as the first author. Half of the multi authored papers in IASLIC Bulletin 2002 have librarians as the first author and two papers are by a group with teachers as the first author and three papers have students as the first author. Five of the seven multiple authored papers in IASLIC Bulletin 2003 had librarians as the first author and two papers had teachers as the first author. Of the 48 many author papers in ILA 2003, 32 are by group of authors headed by librarians, fourteen by teachers as the first author, and in the case of two, students occupy the slot of first author. In the case of ILA 2004, 38 papers are with many author partnerships of which 20 are by librarians as the first author, fifteen by teachers as the first author and three with students as the first author. Thirty four of the forty six papers in SIS 2003 are by librarians as the first author followed by six with teachers as the first author, four by students as the first author and designation of the authors not clear in the case of remaining two papers. Out of the 68 papers through partnerships in SIS 2004, 39 had librarians as the first author, 21 with teachers as the first author, four papers with students as the first author, and rest four papers without designation of the authors.

Of the 351 partnered papers, 216 (62%) had librarians as the second author, 90 (26%) papers with teachers as the second author, and 39 (11%) papers with students as the second author as shown in Table 4. For CALIBER 2003, 22 papers had librarians as the second author, 9 with teachers

Table 3. First Author in Multi-Author Papers

Conference/ Journal	First Author Librarian (P)		Teacher (T)		Student (S)		No Designation		Paper with >1 Author
	#	%	#	%	#	%	#	%	
CALIBER 2003	24	66.67	9	25.00	3	8.33			36
CALIBER Abstracts	7	50.00	5	35.71	2	14.29			14
CALIBER 2004	32	61.54	16	30.77	4	7.69			52
CALIBER Abstracts	7	70.00	2	20.00	1	10.00			10
DBIT 2002	10	90.91	1	9.09					11
DBIT 2003	8	72.73	1	9.09	2	18.18			11
IASLIC B 2002	5	50.00	2	20.00	3	30.00			10
IASLIC B 2003	5	71.43	2	28.57					7
ILA 2003	32	66.67	14	29.17	2	4.17			48
ILA 2004	20	52.63	15	39.47	3	7.89			38
SIS 2003	34	73.91	6	13.04	4	8.69	2	4.35	46
SIS 2004	39	57.35	21	30.88	4	5.88	4	5.88	68
Total	223	63.53	94	26.78	28	7.98	6	1.71	351

as the second author and five papers with students as the second author. Nine of the 14 abstracts provided in the same volume had librarians as the second author, three abstracts had teachers as the second author and in the case of two abstracts students occupy the second author slot. Fifty two papers were published in the conference volume of CALIBER 2004 with author collaboration out of which thirty had librarians as the second author, fifteen with teachers as the second author, and seven with students as the second author. Of the ten collaborated abstracts added, six were written by a group of authors with librarians as the second author, three with teachers as the second author, and one with student as the second author. All the 11 multiple author papers in DBIT 2002 had librarians as the second author and eight out of eleven had the same situation with DBIT 2003 and the remaining three papers had teachers as the second author. Six of the ten papers in IASLIC Bulletin 2002 are written by partnerships involving librarians as the second author and the rest four by teachers as the second author. Three each of the collaborated papers in IASLIC Bulletin 2003 are with teachers and students as the second author and one paper with a teacher as the second author. Of the 48 collaborated papers in ILA 2003, thirty five had librarians in the second author spot, ten with teachers as the second author and the remaining three with students in the second author position. The number of collaborated papers with librarians, teachers and students as the second author for ILA 2004 is respectively 20, 15 and 3. Over 80% of the partnered papers in SIS 2003 are with librarians as the second author and the same in the case of SIS 2004 has come down to 43% where as it showed an increase in the case of teachers from 11% to 26% and for students from 4% to 19%.

The characteristics of authors in the third and still higher orders are highlighted in Table 5. 108 (31%) such papers have librarians as author in the third, fourth, etc., position, twenty five papers with teachers in such position and seven papers have students in the corresponding slot and designations not clear with six papers. Of the sixteen papers with more than two author partnership in CALIBER 2003, nine papers with librarians, four papers with teachers and three papers with students as author at third or higher order position in the author list. In the case of six abstracts involving more than two authors, five are with librarians and one with student in the author list as third/fourth author. Of the thirteen papers in partnership with more than two authors in CALIBER 2004, eleven are with librarians as third author and two with students as the third author. In the case of two abstracts in this category appended in this volume, librarians are at the third author position. Five papers with

Table 4. Second Author in Multi-Author Papers

Conference/ Journal	Second Author Librarian (P) #	%	Teacher (T) #	%	Student (S) #	%	No Designation #	%	Paper with >1 Author
CALIBER 2003	22	61.11	9	25.00	5	13.89			36
CALIBER Abstracts	9	64.28	3	21.43	2	14.28			14
CALIBER 2004	30	57.69	15	28.85	7	13.46			52
CALIBER Abstracts	6	60.00	3	30.00	1	10.00			10
DBIT 2002	11	100.00							11
DBIT 2003	8	72.73	3	27.27					11
IASLIC B 2002	6	60.00	4	40.00					10
IASLIC B 2003	3	42.86	1	14.28	3	42.86			7
ILA 2003	35	72.92	10	20.83	3	6.25			48
ILA 2004	20	52.63	15	39.47	3	7.89			38
SIS 2003	37	80.43	5	10.87	2	4.35	2	4.35	46
SIS 2004	29	42.65	22	32.35	13	19.12	4	5.88	68
Total	216	61.54	90	25.64	39	11.11	6	1.71	351

more than two authors in DBIT 2002 had nine librarians in the third/fourth/fifth author position while three 3-author papers in DBIT 2003 had librarians as the third author. IASLIC Bulletin 2002 had three papers involving partnership of three authors and one paper with four author collaborations of which two with librarians in the third/fourth author slot and three with teachers in a similar position. There are two papers each with three and four authors in IASLIC Bulletin 2003 which together comprise five librarians as third/fourth author and one teacher as third/fourth author. The Proceedings volume of ILA 2003 has twelve three-author papers and three four-author papers and in total there are fifteen librarians as third/fourth and three teachers in the same spot. Of the ten three-author papers in ILA 2004, nine had librarians as the third author and there is a teacher in the same position for one paper. In the case of SIS 2003, there are fifteen papers in three-author partnership and one paper having four authors of which twelve had librarians as third/ fourth author and four papers with teacher as third/fourth author. The maximum number of more than three author partnerships are observed in the case of some papers in SIS 2004 such as eleven papers with three authors each, five papers with four authors each, two papers with five authors in each case, and one paper each with six and nine authors taking the total number of such papers to twenty out of the sixty eight collaborated papers in the conference volume. These papers account a total of twenty six librarians, seven teachers, and three students respectively in the higher order slot.

Table 5. Authors other than First or Second in Multi-Author Papers

Conference/ Journal	Other Author								Paper with >1 Author
	Librarian (P)		Teacher (T)		Student (S)		No Designation		
	#	%	#	%	#	%	#	%	
CALIBER 2003	9	25.00	4	11.11	3	8.33			36
CALIBER Abstracts	5	35.71			1	7.14			14
CALIBER 2004	11	21.15	2	3.85					52
CALIBER Abstracts	2	20.00							10
DBIT 2002	9	81.82							11
DBIT 2003	3	27.27							11
IASLIC B 2002	2	20.00	3	30.00					10
IASLIC B 2003	5	71.43	1	14.28					7
ILA 2003	15	31.25	3	6.25					48
ILA 2004	9	23.68	1	2.63					38
SIS 2003	12	26.08	4	8.69			2	4.35	46
SIS 2004	26	38.24	7	10.29	3	4.41	4	5.88	68
Total	108	30.77	25	7.12	7	1.99	6	1.71	351

The location of authors in collaborated papers is summarized in Table 6. More than 55% of collaborated papers are with authors working in the same institution and another 17% with authors working in different institutions located in the same place. Only 27% of the collaborated papers are written by authors in different institutions in different places. Of the 36 collaborated papers in CALIBER 2003, 19 are from authors working in the same institution followed by 9 papers with authors working in different places affiliated to different institutions. The number of papers from collaboration out of authors working in the same institution is the highest followed by authors working in different places in different institutions and authors working in the same place in different institutions except in the case of SIS 2003.

Table 6. Locations of Authors in Multi-Author Papers

Conference/ Journal	Same Institution		Different Institutions Same Place		Different Institutions Different Places		Papers with >1 author
	#	%	#	%	#	%	
CALIBER 2003	19	52.78	8	22.22	9	25.00	36
CALIBER Abstracts	12	85.71			2	14.28	14
CALIBER 2004	24	46.15	13	25.00	15	28.85	52
CALIBER Abstracts	4	40.00	2	20.00	4	40.00	10
DBIT 2002	7	63.64	1	9.09	3	27.27	11
DBIT 2003	6	54.55	2	18.18	3	27.27	11
IASLIC B 2002	5	50.00	2	20.00	3	30.00	10
IASLIC B 2003	5	71.43			2	28.57	7
ILA 2003	28	58.33	9	18.75	11	22.92	48
ILA 2004	20	52.63	4	10.53	14	36.84	38
SIS 2003	27	58.69	10	21.74	9	19.56	46
SIS 2004	38	55.88	11	16.17	19	27.94	68
Total	195	55.56	62	17.66	94	26.78	351

4. CONCLUSION

Only 44% of the articles are by single authors though the largest number of collaborated papers (38% two-author papers) is still lower than the single author papers. Over 63% of the 276 single author papers are authored by librarians, 25% by teachers, and 8% by students whereas designation of the author is not clear with the remaining 4% papers. As in the case of single author papers, librarians are active as first author in maximum number of collaborated papers (over 63% of collaborated papers have librarian as first author in contrast to 27% of such papers with teachers as first author). Of the 351 partnered papers, 216 (62%) had librarians as the second author, 90 (26%) papers with teachers as the second author, and 39 (11%) papers with students as the second author. 108 (31%) such papers have librarians as author in the third, fourth, etc., position, twenty five papers with teachers in such position and seven papers have students in the corresponding slot and designations not clear with six papers. More than 55% of collaborated papers are with authors working in the same institution and another 17% with authors working in different institutions located in the same place. Only 27% of the collaborated papers are written by authors in different institutions in different places.

The results of the study need to be corroborated with large set of data by including other publications during the same period and later years to verify whether the results can be generalized. Per capita productivity also required to be studied as there are more librarians than teachers to ascertain the increase in publications by librarians is just due to their large number in comparison with teachers. Though students are more than librarians and teachers, most of the students never get the desired grooming to venture into writing research publications. Similar studies maybe conducted regarding trends in older publications to reveal any change in the nature of authorship or affiliations, rural/

urban and metro/city/town divide. Teachers are into teaching and research and they work in partnership with their students and colleagues whereas librarians are supposed to manage the affairs of a library with scholarly activities and publication always taking a back seat. It is a matter of solace for the library profession and librarians that still being so, many librarians strive hard to publish papers as evident from the study.

REFERENCES

1. **CALIBER 2002,** Murthy, T A V et al (ed.), Mapping Technology on Libraries and People, Proceedings of the First International Convention on Automation of Libraries in Education and Research Institutions International (CALIBER) 2003, Ahmedabad, Nirma Education and Research Foundation, 13-15 February 2003, Ahmedabad: INFLIBNET, 2003,xvi, 728 pp.
2. **CALIBER 2003,** Murthy, T A V et al (ed.), Roadmap to New Generation of Libraries Using Emerging Technologies, Proceedings of the Second International Convention on Automation of Libraries in Education and Research Institutions (CALIBER) 2004, Jamia Millia Islamia, New Delhi, 11-13 February 2004, Ahmedabad: Information and Library Network (INFLIBNET) Centre, 2004, ix, 613 pp.
3. **ILA 2003**, Sharma, Pandey, S K et al (ed.), Electronic Information Environment and Library Services A Contemporary Paradigm, Proceedings of the ILA 48th All India Library Conference, Bangalore, 22-25 Jan 2003, Delhi: ILA, 2003, xiv, 938 pp.
4. **ILA 2004,** Rao, Laxman N et al (ed.), Responding to users' need in changing information landscapes: Sojourn of libraries from palm-leaf to palm-top, Seminar papers of 49th All India Library Conference, Bundhelkhand University, Jhansi, 29th Dec, 2003-1st Jan, 2004, Indian Library Association, Delhi, 2004, xvi, 623 pp.
5. **SIS 2003**, Singh, Yogendra et al (ed.), New Challenges in Information Management and E-learning in the age of

Globalisation, Proceedings of Society for Information Science (SIS) 2003 Conference, Roorkee, 9-11 April 2003, Roorkee: Central Library, IIT Roorkee, 2003, 2 vol., (xvi), 770 pp.

6. **SIS 2004**, Chandra, Harish, Pichappan, P, Kundra, Ramesh (ed.), Digital Information Exchange: Pathways to Build Global Information Society, Proceedings of Society for Information Science (SIS) 2004 Conference, Chennai, 22-23 January 2004, Chennai: Central Library, IIT Madras, 2004, xx, 626 pp.
7. **DBIT 2002**, DESIDOC Bulletin of Information Technology, 22 (1-6), 2002, Delhi, DESIDOC.
8. **DBIT 2003**, DESIDOC Bulletin of Information Technology, 23 (1-6), 2003, Delhi, DESIDOC.
9. **IASLIC B 2002**, IASLIC Bulletin, 47 (1-4), 2002, Kolkata, IASLIC.
10. **IASLIC B 2003**, IASLIC Bulletin, 48 (1-4), 2003, Kolkata, IASLIC.

7

PUBLIC LIBRARIES FOR SCIENCE AWARENESS

1. INTRODUCTION

Developing countries would have progressed more, had they have the means to supplement the broadcasting oriented community information communication mechanism to broadcasting plus library centred community information dissemination mechanism and resources to transform their public libraries to at least the level of infrastructure prevailing in their research and higher education libraries. The UNESCO Public Library Manifesto defines the public library as "the local gateway to knowledge, provides a basic condition for lifelong learning, independent decision making and cultural development of the individual and social groups" [2]. It also emphasize that the public library services should be formulated with certain objectives that relate to information, literacy, education and culture in mind such as promoting awareness of cultural heritage, appreciation of the arts, scientific achievements and innovations.

The significant constraints for providing services in public libraries, especially in rural areas, suggested by the

World Information Report, 1997-98, quoted by Dasgupta [4] are:

- The bulk of the population is not information-dependent in day-to-day work and living.
- A large proportion of the population cannot consume information in written form.
- The vast majority of the population does not have the means to access information.
- People in general are not accustomed to pay, cannot pay or are unwilling to pay for information as it does not figure in their list of wants.
- The existing pattern of economic activities does not favour a growth in information consumption.
- The countries do not have sufficient capacity to invest in infrastructure development

Some of the predominant services offered by public libraries in the country are lending out collection of light reading and fiction, reading room facility for newspapers and popular magazines, facility for public viewing of TV programmes, and function as a distribution network for government information like notifications and gazettes. A few of the libraries also hold reference collection and engage in reference services. The problems and constraints faced by the public library system to effectively disseminate information are manifold in the country, essentially as a result of prevailing illiteracy, little money to feed a large number of public libraries, largely dependent on voluntary and not regular professionally trained personnel, and not so positive in taking advantage of latest technology tools and solutions.

Science and Technology (S&T) had a major role to play in the transformation of society but at the same time S&T was getting institutionalised and alienated from the masses; missing the public good component of science [1]. The first

Prime Minister of India, Pandit Jawaharlal Nehru, introduced the concept of modern 'scientific temper' – an enquiring attitude and analytical approach that leads to rational thinking and the pursuit of truth without prejudice [5]. There is also a special provision in the constitution of India "to develop the scientific temper, humanism and spirit of enquiry" [5]. Advocacy and campaigns on issues such as the Silent Valley Project in Kerala, the Bhopal gas disaster and the Narmada dam project have had considerable impact [1] in bringing science awareness to the centre stage. There are also issues like protest of farmers towards genetically modified crops, rural migration to the urban centres in search of better livelihood, environmental concerns, development alienating poorest of the poor, etc. In the new scenario of decision-making getting democratised it is essential that the public is aware of the new developments in science and technology, their advantages and disadvantages [6]. Good or bad, public libraries offer a vast channel of information dissemination centres to effectively disseminate community information which are not tapped to the desired extent even now. A judicious adoption of public libraries as centres for community science information delivery may yield better rewards in the long run though there are advantages and disadvantages in using their wide spread but largely static and not so aggressive network.

2. PUBLIC LIBRARIES

The country presently has 28 states, 6 union territories and the national capital region, which together account for approximately 550 districts. The number of inhabited villages in the country is around 580781 [7] and there is no doubt to imagine the difficulties of facilitating information and library support to the mass of over a billion population, spread over 32 lakhs sq. km. During the last 28 years, the Raja Rammohun Roy Library Foundation (RRRLF) has covered, out of 60000 public libraries located in the country in a scattered way, more than 31000 libraries at different levels [8]. But many of these 60000 libraries are mere reading rooms without many books or other desired elementary infrastructure and trained full time staff. According to International Federation of Library Associations & Institutions (IFLA) standards, there should be one public library for every 3000 people [8], and with over 1 billion people, our country needs more than 343000 public library units which means there may not be even one public library for 8-10 of rural villages.

More villages have high schools than public libraries and with over 98134 higher secondary schools [7] each having at least the namesake of a library. Thus by permitting these libraries to function also as public libraries we are left with at least one library for 3-4 of the rural villages. This is a viable setup considering the geographical terrain of the country, the prevailing infrastructure and the current budgetary constraints. These libraries with the aid of information and communication technology can also function as rural digital libraries and information kiosks to curb the prevailing digital divide in the country between urban and rural areas providing constructive support in science awareness activities.

3. SCIENCE AWARENESS

Science and technology over the last two centuries have changed the way people live, work and survive. Science is not to be treated as a difficult subject taught in schools and colleges but it is to be imbibed for developing a logical thinking process through natural and physical observations which will help in fighting superstition and obscurantism prevailing in the country [9]. The impact of new technologies is bringing tremendous upheavals in traditional societies like ours. You can not think of living without a mobile phone now but still you are amazed that it has gained such a wide popularity in just a decade. Similar is the case with other new technologies like computers, cable television etc. Thus awareness about science, technology and their interfacing and interaction with different activities and issues of society is not of concern to just school children but also the general public. The basic aim of science popularization is to unveil the human face of science so that masses are not afraid of it [10]. Promoting scientific awareness also implies that the awareness leads to scientific information and knowledge being put to good use [11]. Popular science presentation should reveal little about science but enough to make one realise the existence of that science with its entire ramification [10].

Science awareness is getting more crucial due to the visible impacts of globalization and liberalization and emergence of the knowledge economy we live in. Popularisation of science to create a scientific temper among the people is an essential requirement for the development and progress of a country [9]. The Public Science Movement (PSM) groups believe that the public needs to develop a critical understanding of S&T in order to be able to participate in its growth and application, especially in the choice of technologies in different contexts [1]. Gascoigne and Metcalfe enumerate some of the possible measurable objectives of public awareness of science initiatives (PASIs) as the number of high school students completing science courses; science coverage in popular media; movement in the salary levels of scientists and technologists; the number of scientists elected to Parliament; changes in attitudes toward science measured in focus groups and by surveys; the number of people pursuing combined science-economics degrees; the number of high-profile board members holding a B.Sc. or B.E./B.Tech.; the way scientists are depicted in popular films and television shows; and the number of females graduating from universities with a B.Sc. [12].

The 'Science and Technology Policy 2003' details the following about creating public awareness of science and technology [13]:

- There is growing need to enhance public awareness of the importance of science and technology in everyday life, and the directions where science and technology is taking us.
- People must be able to consider the implications of emerging science and technology options in areas which impinge directly upon their lives, including the ethical and moral, legal, social and economic aspects.
- Advances in biotechnology and information technology in recent years have dramatically increased public interest in technology options in wide ranging areas.
- Support for wide dissemination of scientific knowledge, through the support of science museums, planetaria, botanical gardens and the like, be enhanced.
- Every effort must be made to convey to the young the excitement in scientific and technological advances and to instill scientific temper in the population at large.
- Special support provided for programmes that seek to popularize and promote science and technology in all parts of the country.
- Programmes will be developed to promote learning and dissemination of science through the various national languages, to enable effective science communication at all levels.
- A closer interaction of those involved in the natural sciences and technology, social sciences, humanities and other scholarly pursuits to bring about mutual reinforcement, added value and impact.

4. NATIONAL TRENDS

4.1. Media

There exists diverse media for science communication [5]. Science popularisation in India is usually done through print and electronic media [9]. Producing quality software for S&T communication requires a good understanding of the subject matter, creativity and imagination on the part of the producer to ensure that it has the right combination of information and entertainment that will trigger an interest in science [23]. In order to create awareness among illiterates or the newly literate and to maintain the knowledge they acquire folk forms (where print and electronic media suffer due to literacy levels and accessibility) must be used more frequently [5]. The different media largely used for science communication activities in the country include:

Print media: Science publications in book, journal and newspaper format

Audio-visual media: Radio, television, CDs, DVDs

Folk media: puppet shows, street plays, stage performances, folk songs and dances

Interactive media: Science exhibitions, science fairs, Vigyan Jathas, demonstrations, conferences, seminars, workshops, popular science lectures, school science activities, scientific tours, activity kits, and digital software

4.2. Institutions

Various Governmental agencies and non-governmental organisations (NGOs) are involved in science popularisation as also the radio and television channels [9]. Science museums and science centres with their interactive exhibits and hands-on activities provide a viable alternative to other science popularisation programmes [9]. Some institutions and agencies seriously involved in science popularisation and community science awareness initiatives are:

National Council for Science & Technology Communication (NCSTC), founded in 1982, by the Government of India's Department of Science and Technology (DST) has been engaged in science and technology communication / popularisation and inculcation of scientific temper among the people. The chief goals are to create excitement concerning advances in S & T, to enable informed decision-making at the grass roots level, and to encourage intelligent debate on developmental issues. The emphasis has been on development, adaptation, promotion and use of different communication methodologies. Various media, traditional and non-traditional, are being utilised for the purpose, including print, audio/radio, video/TV and folk-forms like songs, dances, street-plays, puppetry etc. Some important activities are research in thrust areas of science and technology communication; development of scripts, films, video and radio programmes, books, slide sets, etc.; short term training for school teachers and activists in science communication; development of science journalists through University Courses; awards and recognition for outstanding science communicators; coordination with state councils and networks of S& T based organisations; developing capacity through science communication; field programmes for demonstrating innovative ideas of science popularisation, outreach and extension activities including National Children's Science Congress, Science Day celebrations, promotion of voluntary blood donation programmes, environmental awareness and positive action, etc. [14]. The NCSTC Network was started in 1991 with the objective of taking science popularisation activities to all the corners of the country. Presently it has around 100 members, including NGOs and government organizations [5]. Efforts of organisations to popularise science have been largely concentrated on school students though the NCSTC and the

Vigyan Prasar tried to focus on other groups as well [11].

Vigyan Prasar is an autonomous organisation setup by the DST in 1989, to undertake large scale science popularisation tasks in the country. They are engaged in publishing, audio video production, popularising HAM radio and astronomy, setting up a National Repository of Science & Technology Videos, radio and TV serials, CD backup of these serials, slide sets, and Solar Eclipse Activity Kit. They have also set up a two way Audio- Video interactive communication network for science communication/ science popularization and disaster management through ISRO's EduSat. Most of the books published by the organisation are being made freely available on the website so as to spread knowledge at the click of a button. Vigyan Prasar Information System (VIPRIS) Clipset is a comprehensive science, technology and environment fortnightly clipping service. VIPNET stands for VIgyan Prasar NETwork - a network to weave all science clubs, societies, organisations (there are 1600 clubs till April 2000) to strengthen the popular science movement in the country. The broad objectives of VIPNET are dissemination of information on S&T; evolution of a holistic approach towards problems through awareness, concern, involvement, and application of the scientific methodology for their resolution; and stimulation of the spirit of curiosity, enquiry, innovation and creativity through activities which would supplement conventional education and make science a very enjoyable and interesting pursuit. All State Science Councils and state DSTs besides the prominent NGOs, have accepted VIPNET as their official network [15].

Natural Resources Data Management System (NRDMS) has been launched by the DST to catalyse the evolution of methodologies and techniques for formulating development strategies. It aims to strengthen S&T inputs in developing tools and techniques for integrated resource management and for capacity building at various levels of planning and implementation in a spatio-temporal context in a multi-level framework. Some of the activities currently undertaken include district GIS database development, software development for management and application of geo-spatial data, hydrology of small watersheds including ground water modeling, bio-geo database and ecological modeling of the Himalayas, mitigation of landslide hazards, coastal zone management and application of information technology for sustainable agriculture production system [16].

Science & Society Division (SSD) of DST has the broad objectives of providing opportunities to motivated scientists and field level workers to take up action oriented and location specific projects aiming towards socio-economic upliftment of poor and disadvantaged sections of the society through appropriate science and technology interventions especially in the rural areas. Some of the initiatives under this programme are long term support to strengthen S&T based voluntary groups as centres of excellence in rural areas; Rural & Women Technology Parks set up for technological empowerment and capacity building of rural poor and women; integrated village development with appropriate S&T intervention and watershed based planning; Technology Intervention for Mountain Eco-systems (TIME) programme for alternative livelihoods in mountain areas including North East; medicinal plants cultivation and processing to benefit SC/ST community; dissemination of state of the art technologies in sericulture for SC/ST communities; programme on improved fodder cultivation to involve and benefit rural women; Bio Integrated Organic Farm Management (BIOFARM) to benefit small and marginal farmers; network NGO's, and research institutions to provide technological solutions to location specific problems etc., [17].

The Indian Science Congress Association (ISCA),

Kolkata holds annual Science Congress inaugurated by the Prime Minister which is regarded as the largest scientific event in the country which has a history of over 90 years. In 1980, the DST sets up a permanent Task Force involving representatives of ISCA and chiefs of different agencies and voluntary organizations chaired by Secretary, DST, for following up various recommendations on the Focal Theme. Every year follow-up actions on recommendations made in the previous Science Congress are discussed at a General Session organized by DST during the Science Congress. Through this process, the Indian Science Congress Association has been contributing to the development of Science in general and National Science Policy, in particular. They also publish a monthly science magazine, Everyman's Science [18].

Homi Bhabha Centre for Science Education (HBCSE) is a National Centre of the Tata Institute of Fundamental Research, Mumbai to promote equity and excellence in science and mathematics education from primary school to undergraduate college level, and encourage the growth of scientific literacy in the country. They publish popular science books and hold mobile exhibitions to inculcate a developmental and human view of science among students, teachers and lay public [19].

National Council of Science Museums (NCSM) is the largest network of science centres / museums under a single umbrella in the world. The NCSM science centers /museums located in 25 different sites in India have a total floor area of 150683 sq mtrs., and have been visited by around 6.4 million people during 2006-07. A visit to these museums by going through the various exhibits rekindles human being's natural and nascent interest in science [20].

All-India People's Science Network (AIPSN): Bharat Gyan Vigyan Samiti (BGVS) or All India People's Science Network (AIPSN) is a grassroots organization having volunteers and workers in most of the states of India [21]. At the first All-India People's Science Conference (AIPSC) in 1988, the All-India People's Science Network (AIPSN), a loose coalition of people's science groups around the country, was formed. Today, the AIPSN comprises 40 organisations in 22 States committed to the use of science to promote equitable and sustainable development reaching an estimated 18,000 villages spread over 300 districts [1].

State Science and Technology Programmes: State Science & Technology Councils have been set-up in all the States and Union Territories. Several States have also formed a separate Department of Science & Technology. DST played a catalytic role by facilitating the State Governments in establishing and developing the State S&T Councils and by providing support for their technical secretariats. DST in collaboration with respective State Councils identify activity-areas for promotion of technology models for-rural application as well as development of location specific need based technologies such as cupola furnaces, rice shellers and induction furnaces, solar energy for day lighting and space heating purposes, defluoridation of drinking water, pedal operated rice mill, leg operated wool spinning charkha, mushroom cultivation, reverse osmosis desalination plant, and environment friendly disposal of plastics and hospital waste [22].

PSM groups have engaged in developing and encouraging people-centred technologies that are less capital intensive and empower a large number of people, workers, crafts persons and artisans. Some examples of such initiatives are: wireless in local loop for telecommunications, the simputer and village information software, bio-mass as replacement for cement/concrete in civil constructions, windmills and bio-mass based energy systems, non-chemical inputs to boost agricultural productivity, improved small-scale mechanised looms, small-scale oil presses and other food processing units, and mechanised black smithy [1].

There are state level science popularization and science for society initiatives like the Banga Vigyan Parishad, the Kerala Shastra Sahitya Parishad (KSSP), the Marathi Vigyan Parishad, the Assam Science Society, the Tamil Nadu Science Forum, the Karnataka Rajya Vigyan Parishad, the Jan Vigyan Vedika of Andhra Pradesh, the Pondicherry Science Forum, the Madhya Pradesh Vigyan Sabha, the Himachal Gyan Vigyan Samiti etc.

4.3. Programmes

Activities and programmes undertaken by the respective institutions are discussed in the section above. Anniversaries of scientists, institutes, organisations and societies, including the World Health Day, etc., can be celebrated; discussions and debates with the concerned scientists organised; and doors of concerned laboratories and organisations thrown open to masses and media [10]. Another very popular and important programme has been the 'scientific explanation of miracles' using trained science 'activists' to demonstrate and explain so-called miracles [5]. There are certain awards for science popularisation: NCSTC National Award for Best S & T Coverage in the Mass Media, INSA Indira Gandhi Award for science popularisation, and B.C. Deb Memorial Award of the Indian Science Congress Association. Some programmes undertaken for creating better awareness of science among general public are:

Vigyan Jathas: Vigyan Jathas convey to the people what needs to be conveyed in the language they can understand and at a pace in which they can assimilate that information [6]. Twenty-six people's science groups came together and organised the nation-wide Bharat Jan Vigyan Jatha (BJVJ) in October-November 1987 with the support of the DST which was followed by the first All-India People's Science Conference (AIPSC), which was held in Kannur in

Kerala in 1988 [1]. The Bharat Jan Vigyan Jatha (BJVJ) of 1987 was the largest science communication experiment done anywhere in the world and based on its success, another Jatha, Bharat Jan Gyan Vigyan Jatha (BJGVJ) was conducted in 1992, combining literacy campaign with scientific awareness programme [11]. Jathas were also conducted as part of the Year of Scientific Awareness (YSA), 2004.

Year of Scientific Awareness (YSA): Spreading awareness among the people about the scientific aspects of the issues confronting them and inculcating in them the habit of solving these issues through community action are the main objectives for observing 2004 as the Year of Scientific Awareness (YSA).

Vigyan Rail: As part of YSA, "Vigyan Rail", a train containing exhibits on Indian S&T efforts was flagged off by the Prime Minister on December 15, 2003, from Safdarjung Railway Station in New Delhi and sent to the different regions of the country to create science awareness among the children and general public.

Science through Art: Science propagators are more convinced that they have to adopt local languages, local idioms, local culture, popular art forms, folk literature and art, etc. to achieve more success in the way science is taken to the masses.

Children's Science Congress: This is a programme involving children in the age group of 10 - 17 years, from all over the country, to encourage them to relate learning of science to the environment around; to know their immediate social and physical environment and provide them a forum to interact with scientists to quench their curiosity and creativity. The Congress has been organised in almost all districts every year with more and more schools joining the activity. National events are held since 1993.

A list of few interesting events related to science popularisation in the country is highlighted in Table 1.

Table 1. Landmark events in creating Science Awareness

Year	Event
1914	The first meeting of the Science Congress was held from January 15-17 at the premises of the Asiatic Society, Calcutta
1938	The Silver Jubilee Session of the Science Congress was held at Calcutta
1963	The Science Congress celebrated its Golden Jubilee at Delhi
1973	The Diamond Jubilee Session of the Science Congress was held at Chandigarh in January 3-9
1978	National Council of Science Museums (NCSM), an autonomous society under the Ministry of Culture, Government of India was formed on April 4
1982	Department of Science and Technology (DST) set up the National Council for Science and Technology Communication (NCSTC)
1987	The Bharat Jan Vigyan Jatha
1988	Platinum Jubilee of Science Congress. The first All-India People's Science Conference (AIPSC)
1988	All-India People's Science Network (AIPSN)
1989	Vigyan Prasar
1992	The Bharat Jan Gyan Vigyan Jatha
1993	Annual Children's Science Congress started
2004	Year of Scientific Awareness (YSA-2004) and Vigyan Chetna Jathas under YSA-2004

5. ROLE OF PUBLIC LIBRARIES

Salwi has underlined that the supplementing media for science awareness should be made available in public libraries [10]. We have seen that most of the science awareness initiatives are undertaken either through various arms of the Government or through NGOs and science clubs. Raja Rammohun Roy Library Foundation (RRRLF) may interact with these institutions as the apex body of public libraries for these social service institutions to get their rightful share in this pious effort. Some of the activities public libraries can initiate are:

1. Having copies of all popular science publications in the collection. Preference must be given to those publications in regional and local languages
2. A small multimedia center to view audio video collection of popular science publications
3. TV and Radio facility to view and listen to science programmes. The libraries may announce in advance the schedule of these programmes to gather the attention of more members of the community. They should also arrange follow up meetings either before or after such broadcasts with local experts like school teachers so that nuances of the topic are better understood
4. Public libraries should celebrate certain important national and international events (or days) that would generate widespread awareness in the society, such as National Science Day (28 February), National Safety Day (4 March), National Immunisation Day (16 March), World Disabled Day (19 March), World Forestry Day (21 March), World Health Day (7 April), World Earth Day (22 April), International Energy Day (3 May), World Telecom Day (17 May), World No Tobacco Day (31 May), World Environment Day (5 June), World Population Day (11 July), International Literacy Day (8 September), World Habitat Day (7 Oct.), World Food Day (16 Oct.), World Aids Day (1 Dec.), National Energy Conservation Day (14 Dec.), to name a few.
5. Public library may organise events related to science such as popular lectures, folk shows, drama, adaptation of subject matter covered in popular science books for the consumption of people who can

not digest the content otherwise etc., as part of local festivals. We are yet to make a dent in wiping out superstitions, particularly in tribal areas where literacy levels are low and the general public is still largely ignorant about common scientific principles, such as the fact that the Earth orbits the Sun [5].

6. There should be information communication technology enabled portal for meeting the local information needs in the public library where public would get information of interest related to their health, education, and livelihood.
7. Collaborative programmes and extension activities with local schools, science clubs and cultural associations in creating awareness and arriving at social priorities for issues concerning the population.
8. Some facility for archiving (either digital or analogue) radio and TV programmes related to science popularization may be made available in public libraries so that anyone can watch these at their convenience. There are also exclusive science cable channels like Discovery, Animal Planet, National Geographic and science programmes are also beamed in other channels. There will be a provision for translating, archiving and distributing these to public libraries. This work can not be undertaken by individual public libraries but only by state central libraries, bigger public libraries or private agencies with the support of RRRLF.

6. PROBLEMS IN SPREADING SCIENCE AWARENESS

Patairiya foresees the following difficulties in science communication efforts [5]:

- Radio, which is extremely popular in rural areas, has an increasing amount of scientific content than television

- While literacy levels are increasing (around 52 %), scientific literacy is still drastically low
- Given the country's large population, limited resources and multitude of languages, mass science education faces particularly great challenges
- Without more attention on local languages, much of the population will miss out on science communication efforts

Salwi presents the following issues for the betterment of science communication in the country [10]:

- Science writing is more of an art rather than a science and due to the present lack of emphasis on the art aspect of science popularisation has suffered to date.
- The human side of science is totally neglected in popular science presentations.
- Inability of science communicators to distinguish between technical report writing and popular science writing.
- While writing a popular science article on a subject one often needs the assistance of a scientist doing research in that very subject. But in India the scientist of the concerned subject is often not available for consultation and as a result writings lack the necessary quality, verve and colour.

The major impediments of general population with respect to science awareness are:

Information Drought: Lack of availability of information resources in their level and style of interest

Literacy: Low literacy rate and poor educational background

Time: They are so busy with household and livelihood, so that they don't get time for entertainment, reading, or accessing information.

Language: There are many languages and even in one place more than one language is spoken. Even the same language is spoken differently in different places in a state. More over, the information required might not be available in the language in which one is proficient. We need good language representation and translation mechanisms to get over this problem.

Culture: Due to the prevailing mindset and cultural barriers, rural people are unable to seek and gather information for their livelihood unlike their counterparts in urban areas. The situation will be more volatile in the case of those termed inferior in caste and creed, minorities, women and children.

Bad shape of public libraries and their alienation from the development model: Where to find funds for a total overhaul of public libraries to supplement the broadcasting oriented development paradigm to a broadcasting plus library centred community information dissemination mechanism and transform public libraries at least to the level of infrastructure prevailing in our research and higher education libraries is the big question.

Poor use of ICT: Infrastructure limitations prevent the required information to reach the needy.

Media Coverage: On average, science only accounts for around three per cent of coverage by India's mass media [5]. Editors of newspapers should ensure that more and more science journalists are recruited and adequate space is provided for science coverage [11]. Science writing still tends to be dry and boring, making it unsurprising that few science articles interest newspapers and magazines and the number of capable science communicators and voluntary scientific organisations is alarmingly low hardly sufficient to cater to the country's large and diverse population [5]. Cable and television are not used to the desired extent for science awareness programmes (radio is an exception up to some extent) as the popular media are too biased towards sports and movie/serial based entertainment, which gather more advertisement revenues. Sehgal opined that the coverage has been good in respect of the agricultural sector, highlighting Indian efforts but most of the coverage in other disciplines is based on the work being carried on in other countries due to the difficulties of getting this information from laboratories/institutions [11]. There are signs that interest in science communication is waning in the print media [5]. Newspapers are not reluctant to cover S & T but the inflow of information has been inadequate [23].

7. CONCLUSION

The infrastructure and financial support of public libraries and society's interest in them have to be visibly improved for engaging them for constructive science awareness programmes. The number of science clubs may not cross even five thousand-not large enough for this vast country with a population of almost one billion whereas we have a more than a lakh public and higher/senior secondary school libraries together. Thus a library has more reach to the public and by the very nature of their existence and activities; they may be extended to support science promotion activities. The media frenzy world we live in needs the citizens to be more aware of what is happening around us and public libraries emerge as social catalysts in unbiased provision of information for various societal needs turning citizens more informed. It is not possible to have a fully science literate society [10]. The efforts of the PSM are becoming more relevant today as the adverse impact of liberalisation and globalisation is felt increasingly by the ordinary people and the state is gradually abdicating its responsibilities in education, employment, health and social welfare [1]. Initiatives from government institutions, NGOs, science clubs, PSMs, etc., will no doubt receive a major boost for eradicating the evils in society, for achieving better health, environment and literacy for its citizens, and for fighting superstitions by involving public libraries in the people's science information dissemination network and streamlining their catalytic role for science awareness.

REFERENCES

1. Ramachandran, R., The messengers of science, Frontline, Volume 21 - Issue 03, January 31 - February 13, 2004, http://www.hinduonnet.com/fline/fl2103/stories/20040213004211400.htm.
2. UNESCO Public Library Manifesto, www.ifla.org/documents/libraries/policies/ unesco.htm
3. Dasgupta, Kalpana. Libraries and librarians in India on the threshold of the 3rd millennium: challenges and risks, 66th IFLA Council and General Conference, Jerusalem, Israel, 13-18 August, http://www.ifla.org/IV/ifla66/papers/039-120e.htm
4. World Information Report 1997/98, Paris: UNESCO, 1997 (quoted by Dasgupta).
5. Patairiya, Manoj, Science communication in India: perspectives and challenges, SciDev.Net, 20 March 2002, http://www.scidev.net/opinions/index.cfm?fuseaction=readopinions&itemid=47& langauge=1
6. Ramamurthi, V.S. Taking issues to the people (Interview), Frontline, Volume 21 - Issue 03, January 31 - February 13, 2004, http://www.hinduonnet.com/fline/ fl2103/stories/20040213004810800.htm.
7. Manorama Year Book 1999, Kottayam, Malayala Manorama.
8. Bhattacharjee, R. Public Library Services in India: Systems and Deficiencies, Country Report: India, http://www.ifla.org/VII/s8/annual/cr02-in.htm
9. Ganguly, T.K. Calcutta Science City: A Landmark in Popularising Science, http://pib.nic.in/feature/fe0599/f2005991.html
10. Salwi, Dilip M. Science Popularisation and some Unrealised

Aspects, Indian Journal of Science Communication, 1(1), January - June, 2002, http://www.iscos.org/ vol1/rp3.htm.

11. Sehgal, Narender K. The thrust is on popularising science (interview), Frontline, Volume 21 - Issue 03, January 31 - February 13, 2004 http://www.hinduonnet.com/ fline/ fl2103/stories/20040213005311000.htm
12. Gascoigne, T., and Metcalfe, J. Why do governments spend money on national programs of science awareness? Paper presented at the sixth International Conference on Public Understanding of Science and Technology, February 1-3, 2001, Geneva. (Quoted by Edwards, Christopher, Evaluating European Public Awareness of Science Initiatives A Review of the Literature, Science Communication, Vol. 25 No. 3, March 2004, 260-271)
13. Science and Technology Policy 2003, Department of Science and Technology, Govt. of India, http://dst.gov.in/stsysindia/ stp2003.htm
14. National Council for Science & Technology Communication (NCSTC), Department of Science and Technology, Govt. of India, http://dst.gov.in/scientific-programme/s-t_ncstc.htm
15. Vigyan Prasar, http://www.vigyanprasar.gov.in/
16. Natural Resources Data Management System (**NRDMS**), Department of Science and Technology, Govt. of India, http:/ /dst.gov.in/scientific-programme/s-t_nrdms.htm
17. Science and Society Program (SSP), Department of Science and Technology, Govt. of India, http://dst.gov.in/scientific-programme/s-t_ssp.htm
18. Indian Science Congress Association (ISCA), http:// www.sciencecongress.org/
19. Homi Bhabha Centre for Science Education (HBCSE), http:/ /www.hbcse.tifr.res.in/
20. National Council of Science Museums (NCSM), http:// ncsm.gov.in/
21. Bharat Gyan Vigyan Samiti (BGVS) or All India People's Science Network (AIPSN), http://www.bgvs.org/rubrique39. html

22. State Science & Technology Programme, Department of Science and Technology, Govt. of India, http://dst.gov.in/scientific-programme/s-t_scst.htm
23. Padmanabhan, B.S. Science for social progress, Frontline, Volume 21 - Issue 09, April 24 - May 07, 2004, http://www.hinduonnet.com/fline/fl2109/stories/20040507003409900.htm

8

Public Libraries and Digital Initiatives

1. INTRODUCTION

The Public Library Manifesto of UNESCO emphasizes that the public library services should be formulated with certain objectives that relate to information, literacy, education and culture in mind such as [1]:

- creating and strengthening reading habits in children from an early age;
- supporting both individual and self conducted education as well as formal education at all levels;
- providing opportunities for personal creative development;
- stimulating the imagination and creativity of children and young people;
- promoting awareness of cultural heritage, appreciation of the arts, scientific achievements and innovations;
- providing access to cultural expressions of all performing arts;

- fostering inter-cultural dialogue and favouring cultural diversity;
- supporting the oral tradition;
- ensuring access for citizens to all sorts of community information;
- providing adequate information services to local enterprises, associations and interest groups;
- facilitating the development of information and computer literacy skills;
- supporting and participating in literacy activities and programmes for all age groups, and initiating such activities if necessary

National Knowledge Commission made the following recommendations for public library collections [5]:

- The size and nature of the collection should reflect the local requirements.
- Locally relevant language material should be available.
- Book purchase should be a continuous process and at least 10% of the book collection should be less than five years old.
- At least 60% of the library's budget should be spent on collection development.

Ranganathan formulated an integrated five-tier public library system comprising primary service library, secondary service library (city central and district central libraries), tertiary service library (state central library), national library and the futuristic world grid of public libraries [6]. This largely acted as the guiding principle in evolving public library system in the country. Depending on whether the Public Library Act is in vogue and based on the interests of the State Government or the level of public movement behind this cause, there may be variations across states on the penetration and depth of public library network and services. Some of the predominant services offered by public libraries in India are lending out collection of light reading and fiction, reading room facility for newspapers and popular magazines, acting as a dissemination network for government information like notifications and gazettes. Some of them also hold reference collection and engage in reference services. The problems and constraints faced by the public library system to effectively disseminate information are manifold in the country, essentially as a result of:

- A considerable percentage of the population is illiterate or functionally literate forcing typical library resources and services to be of minimal use to them
- Poor allocation for the infrastructure improvement and collection development of public libraries
- Lack of enough sanctioned professional positions, forcing most of the services to be operated by voluntary non-professional staff, causing sufficient deterioration on the quality of information organisation and services
- There is also a problem of educated professionals preferring to work in special and academic libraries than public libraries severely impacting the quality and quantity of public library services
- Little emphasis on adoption Information Technology in public library systems and services

Being a State responsibility as per the Constitution, states are vested with the mandate to set up public libraries at different levels. The state governments have departments/directorates/councils of public libraries to start, maintain and operate public libraries under its jurisdiction. But due to the difference in the level of development of public libraries in different states, the Department of Culture, Government of India has set up Raja

Rammohun Roy Library Foundation (RRRLF) to act as a nodal agency for development of public libraries in India. Since all the States have not passed the requisite library legislation, RRRLF is working towards a model Public Library Bill. The RRRLF has also been given the responsibility of resource mobilization for modernization of the state and district central libraries, the development of infrastructure and training of personnel [9].

2. PUBLIC LIBRARY SYSTEM

During the last 28 years, the Raja Rammohun Roy Library Foundation (RRRLF) has covered, out of 60000 public libraries located in the country in a scattered way, more than 31000 libraries [2]. But many of these 60000 libraries (see Table 1) are mere reading rooms without much books or good infrastructure or trained full time staff. According to International Federation of Library Associations & Institutions (IFLA) standards, there should be one public library for every 3000 people [2], and with over 1 billion people, our country needs more than 343000 public library units which means there may not be even one public library for 8-10 of rural villages.

Since there are more secondary schools (98134 as per 1995-96 data [11] and we presume that a library exists in at least schools in this higher level) than public libraries, it a viable and pragmatic proposition to utilize libraries of these schools also to serve the general public beyond school hours. How many of these secondary schools are located in rural areas is not clear. Thus using the existing public and secondary school libraries, we are left with at least one library for 3-4 of the rural villages as a viable setup considering the geographical terrain of the country, the prevailing infrastructure and the current budgetary allocation. These libraries with the aid of information and communication technology can function as rural digital libraries and information kiosks to curb the prevailing digital divide in the country between urban and rural areas.

Table 1. Public Library System

Public Libraries	Covered by RRRLF [2]	Total (Approximate) [2]
State Central Libraries	28	35
Divisional and District Libraries	451	597
Sub-Divisional/Taluka/Tehsil Libraries	501	2300
Town & Rural Libraries	29820	Town- 15000, Rural-42000
Nehru Yuvak Kendras	272	500
Jawahar Bal Bhavans	49	120
Others	128	
	31249	60000

3. PUBLIC LIBRARY SERVICES

Gardner estimated the use patterns of the Central Library of Delhi Public Library and found that 28.89% of the users have less than 16 years of age, 26.67% in between 17-20 years, 30.35% around 21-29 years, 9.65% about 30-45 years and only 2.47% have above 45 years. The educational attributes are 21.27% users primary school, 18.36% middle school, 28.59% matriculation, 10.54% intermediate, 10.14% graduate, 1.81% postgraduate and 2.05% professionals. Out of these only 31.28% of the users reside farther than 1.5 miles from the library [12].

Users of public libraries often require a variable mix of information generated by Government, media, NGOs, rural development practitioners and experts, oral and written indigenous rural knowledge passed on to generations largely through informal means, statistical information, implementation data from previous projects and schemes, etc. The sources include published and unpublished, formal and informal, print and non-print etc. The second constraint raises enough justification for the necessity of information in non-written forms like audio, video, and multimedia. The advent of computer and information technology has yielded the availability of all these forms into one computer amenable form. Perhaps that is the reason why we should explore the adoption of these new technologies for delivering public library services to a large mass of illiterate and semiliterate populace, apart from improving the services presently provided to the reading public.

The American Center [7] and British Council [8] libraries falling in the genre of public libraries in the country would be able to provide many distinctive services as a result of:

- Assimilation of the state of the art practices and technology for information work
- Result oriented and service driven management
- Their clientele, being the upper crust of the Indian society who are able to pay slightly higher service charges and more responsive to access the sophisticated facilities
- Continuous weeding out of collection (though the total collection being small) ensures relevance and higher use rate
- Better pay and service conditions lure the best professionals in India to work for them

Public libraries adopting similar practices may be able to perform more effectively in their social development goals.

4. DIGITAL INITIATIVES

Digital libraries aim at unhindered access to content over computer and communication networks. Our libraries are getting seriously engaged in the development of prototypes of digital information resources, being influenced by developments in the developed countries. Libraries hope to achieve the following as a result of digitization:

- content which lie inaccessible or less used in its present physical form can be put to more visible and enhanced use
- overcome the limitations of few number of copies in the case of heavily used content
- provide a hypertext approach laden with multimedia features
- simulate learning by doing
- sustain attention and interest of the user for long duration

The static content in printed sources fails to attract users who are increasingly exposed to the widely appealing features of new broadcasting technologies and IT intensive presentation tools. Multimedia enabled digital information will also make it consumable to a large percentage of illiterate and old population. With a comparatively strong IT workforce and the emerging development oriented governance, it is not difficult to set up rural digital libraries to create, collect and host information of interest to the rural community as a major initiative to improve the rural livelihood.

Attempting an exhaustive list of techno social projects is beyond the scope of this discussion as many projects and initiatives are happening in different parts of the country and many of them are similar in content and scope.

Each such project illustrates viable application of information communication technologies. Some of these initiatives give enough hints about what are the components of a digital library facility of use to ordinary people. A digital 'public library' must essentially facilitate to provide easy and convenient access to:

- Single window system to provide and seek different G2C (Government to Citizen), C2G, G2G, C2C services
- Facility for computer or other mode of archiving and retrieving programmes on public welfare aired on radio and beamed on television or cable channels
- access to electronic books, electronic periodicals and electronic databases
- information about government schemes, rural market, etc.
- e-learning facilities of rural children and continuing education facilities for rural adults
- Subject gateways and virtual libraries
- Born digital in-house publications from the village or for the village
- Written or voice communication through local language email inside the village or among nearby villages
- Government publications, spiritual, heritage and folklore resources, etc.

In addition to functioning as a digital library, it should also replicate itself as a village information kiosk and communication facility in an interactive mode as a single window facility to satisfy the practical information needs of rural population.

5. IT FOR PUBLIC LIBRARY WORK

The National Knowledge Commission suggests networking of approximately 54,000 public libraries in existence should be undertaken in a phased manner and should be completed by 2011 under the aegis of RRRLF by ensuring state-of-the-art technology storage, dissemination and replication of the data through mirror sites, gateways, portals, and inter-library loan facilities [5]. The Commission recommends open source web-enabled library management software supporting multiple Indian language scripts/ dialects should be developed if necessary and provided to all public libraries for facilitating networking [5]. Matoria et al briefs about the e-granthalaya software freely distributed for libraries by National Informatics Centre, New Delhi [13]. NewGenLib [14], library automation software developed in the country is currently available as an open source tool for library automation. Similarly there are other open source library automation packages like Koha [10] and Evergreen [4]. These packages help public libraries to automate their collections in a cost effective manner.

The Department of Culture through the Central Secretariat Library (CSL) has laid down standards for library development software and networking as well as for bibliographic description to ensure standardization both in infrastructural development as well as retro-conversion of library catalogue in machine-readable format [9]. Similar exercises were also conducted by several library networks and perhaps the public library movement can seriously think of accepting one or many such systems for their in-house data management. The onus of creating and maintaining databases can be assigned to the vast spectrum of public libraries, may be first up to taluka level and later on can be passed on to all the individual libraries depending up on the penetration of technology and staff expertise in them. Since the collection and other resources are duplicated, data management at any level will not be a problem, if efforts will be put on formulating guidelines on authority control and data validation. May be all libraries in one taluka can host the same union catalogue with proper identification of the individual holdings guiding even the user of a title demanded to the nearest holding. RRRLF is having matching grant schemes for "assistance to state, central and district Libraries to acquire TV-cum-VCR sets and cassettes for educational purposes, and assistance to libraries below the district level for increasing accommodation" [3]. Some of these schemes could be extended or modified to frame similar schemes for computer and communications infrastructure in public libraries; they may be provided computers with broadband internet connectivity. This is all the more essential since many of the state governments are pursuing an enthusiastic agenda towards migrating to e-governance and making the administration and welfare measures more open, deep and transparent.

A possible framework for taking advantage of digital initiatives happening in the country through public libraries is shown in figure 1. The figure proposes public library as the rural community hub for accessing information in electronic form facilitating interactivity and contacting experts. Some areas which gain immediate attention through this scheme is information and resources concerning health care, education (especially distance learning and e-learning), vocational skills and employability, livelihood, and career opportunities.

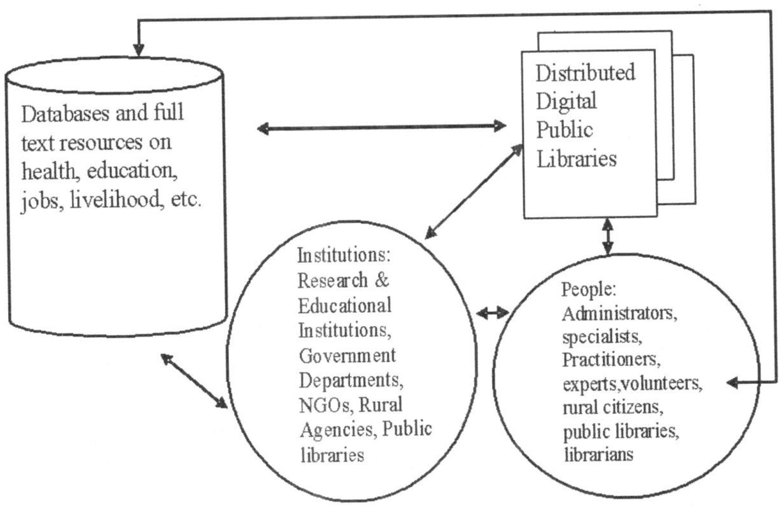

Fig. 1. Public Library and Digital Services

6. CONCLUSION

Information, communication and Entertainment (ICE) and their convergence are manifesting in diverse forms to touch our lives. Open source movement and public libraries emerging as repositories of local content would contribute substantially in overcoming the age old passive feature of public libraries. Since public libraries being the nerve centres for spreading socio-cultural information that can be used for improving the quality of life, much needs to be done in restructuring the programmes and plans for upgrading the public library system in the country. What is needed is a changing mindset to redevelop public libraries as a 'beyond book' social service centre and knowledge centre to take care of the diverse educational, healthcare, vocational and other information requirements of the local community at large. Let public libraries restructured as network kiosks to deliver and access print and non-print information facilities and support services would be the first point to tap the digital initiatives happening in the country.

REFERENCES

1. UNESCO Public Library Manifesto, www.ifla.org/documents/libraries/policies/ unesco.htm
2. Bhattacharjee, R., Public Library Services in India: Systems and Deficiencies, Country Report: India, http://www.ifla.org/VII/s8/annual/cr02-in.htm
3. Raja Rammohan Roy Library Foundation, Calcutta, http://216.87.26.241/en/org/ raja%20 ram.htm
4. http://open-ils.org/
5. http://knowledgecommission.gov.in/downloads/recommendations/LibrariesAnnex.pdf
6. Ranganathan, S R, Integrated Public Library System, pp. 208-212, in Public Library System, ed. by S R Ranganathan and A Neelameghan.
7. http://americanlibrary.in.library.net

8. http://library.britishcouncil.org.in/librarynetwork.asp
9. Dasgupta, Kalpana, Libraries and librarians in India on the threshold of the 3rd millennium: challenges and risks, 66th IFLA Council and General Conference, Jerusalem, Israel, 13-18 August, http://www.ifla.org/IV/ifla66/papers/039-120e.htm
10. http://www.koha.org/
11. Manorama Year Book 1999, Kottayam, Malayala Manorama.
12. Gardner, Frank M., The Delhi Public Library: An Evaluation Report, Zurich, UNESCO, 1957, pp. 26-29.
13. Matoria, Ram Kumar, Upadhyay, P.K., Moni, Madaswamy, Automation and networking of public libraries in India using the e-Granthalaya software from the National Informatics Centre, Program: electronic library and information systems, 41(1), 2007, pp. 47 - 58
14. http://www.newgenlib.com/

9

Digital Libraries and Ranganathan

1. INTRODUCTION

S R Ranganthan, the doyen of Library Science left for his heavenly abode well before computer and information technology impacting the library scene in the country. However like every master and genius in any field of knowledge, the impact and influence of his ideas continue to reflect in the years to come. He was also sympathetic and accepting to the idea of computer as a tool for advancing librarianship as evident from his statement that "World War II ushered in the Electronic Age into the world. The Computer is one of the versatile forms in which Electronics can help mankind. We must accept the computer. We must derive all the benefits it is capable of giving us" [1]. He had the intuition to wonder at what future may hold for the growing organisms of libraries "what further stages are in store for this GROWING ORGANISM- the library- we can not anticipate fully. Who knows that a day may not come when the dissemination of knowledge, which is the vital function of libraries, will be realized even by means other than those of the printed book?" [2]. What a perfect forecast considering the impact electronic resources and non print resources are making in today's hybrid libraries!

2. DIGITAL LIBRARIES VS RANGANATHAN'S IDEAS

The vision document of 'Digital Library of India' highlights the need of digital libraries and digital archiving as: shortcomings of print archives; many works are rare; accessibility limited to a certain population or location; threats to paper archives like wanton act of destruction; and contrary to the popular beliefs, the libraries, museums, and publishers do not routinely maintain broadly comprehensive archives [3].

Digital libraries aim at providing ease of access to information resources (both macro and micro thought) in digital form at the desktop through intranet/internet. Information is put in digital form for use and enhancing its use. Every user of digital library is presented with content of interest to satisfy his/her information needs. Digital library also unravels the information resources in its base to interested users by providing various search options and interfaces maximizing the usage of content stored in digital mode. Search, locate and access through digital mode is faster than those through the print mode. Every technology innovation and social development touching and transforming library science and library is a clear illustration of the fact that library is a growing organism. Digital libraries are just one more reflection of this universal truth.

Digital libraries not only advance the ideals of Ranganthan's laws, principles and practices of providing ease of access at the desktop to all users who want information and all information stored for access but also provide new areas for testing his principles and applying his contributions.

Ranganathan identified that the unit of service should be an individual article in a periodical or a section and even a paragraph in a book [4]; it cannot any longer be macro thought; it must be nascent micro thought in the research sphere [4]. Efficient, prompt, pin-pointed, exhaustive service of nascent micro thought to specialists necessitated by the social pressure of today [4] may be achieved by supplementing the printed information base in more ways than one by the digital libraries.

3. SOME FOCUS AREAS

3.1. A better organised Web

It is not only the terms indexed but the context provided to the terms when mapped with a discipline or area of research leads to better retrieval. What we face in web search now is a flood of retrievals discouraging users to identify useful references; separating quality from the massive quantify is often a very tedious exercise. The popularity of various "free" resources like Google and Yahoo has often drowned out the authoritative and authentic information [5]. Facets make a multi-dimensional organizational scheme, and web browsers are an easy and familiar tool for navigating many dimensions. All of the benefits of faceted classifications can be realized on the web [6]. Perhaps the principles of classification and facets proposed by Ranganathan and other library scientists may play a pivotal role in enabling "efficient, prompt, pin-pointed, exhaustive service of nascent micro thought to specialists" [4].

Gnoli calls for a synthesis between library classification perspectives and computer-based indexing and retrieval to obtain both powerful and effective organization of large amounts of information in any form [7]. A survey of the literature on applying facets on the web [6] shows that librarians think it a good idea but are unsure how to do it, while the web people who are already doing it are often unaware of S.R. Ranganathan, the Classification Research Group, and the decades of history behind facets [8].

Considering Ranganathan's complex notation scheme developed for the Colon Classification, as well as his principles of facet analysis as applied to the organization of digital information, Glassel remarked that he was a Yahoo!. Each term in a Yahoo! notation string contains individual words which have meaning on their own, but once combined with other words into a string, a context is created, providing a deeper meaning much like a faceted classification [9]. Long-term solutions to the problems of indexing the Web will probably involve multiple overlapping methods of classifying and indexing knowledge, so that people coming from every possible angle can find their way to resources that work best for them [10].

3.2. Web belongs to librarians too

Like the expertise needed for the application and use of technology, there is a parallel expertise needed about collecting, organizing and embedding information successfully in information systems, presenting it intelligently in interfaces, and providing search capabilities that effectively exploit the statistical characteristics of information and human information seeking behavior [10]. As information managers with a track record of managing printed resources for ages, librarians and their expertise would definitely go a long way in ensuring the onset of a more user friendly and information friendly web. What is needed for documents on the web is a tool that provides a standard framework for developers to fill-in as a subject heading to produce an organizing sequence when sorted using the assigned subject heading as key as well as provide the necessary search terms to provide access [12].

3.3. Modifying library routines

The user should not be constrained to a selection of

available information that is "book-bound," "publisher-bound," or even "subject-bound" so that information should be organized for self-directed and learner-empowered inquiries [5]. Libraries help the users to locate books and monographs in their collection from own OPACs whereas when the question of searching of journal article comes, the user is directed to electronic databases/indexing and abstracting journals. Same is the case with e-resources which are not even properly entered into catalogue records or holdings information. Cloonan and Dove thus called "closed stacks" or "The Invisible Library"—electronic resources hidden from users because they are not fully integrated into the many pathways by which readers look for information [5]. They propose adding proper MARC records to the catalog; providing good integration with teachers' class pages from learning management systems; making good use of metasearch and link-resolving tools; and enabling contextual linking from library site pages and subject guides to make electronic open stacks.

To achieve these objectives, the influence of Ranganathan and his contributions play not smaller a role than the contributions of current researchers. Bates remarked that faceted classification is to hierarchical classification as relational databases are to hierarchical databases [10]. Ranganathan's principles of facet analysis had come from a man ahead of his time [9].

Ranganthan viewed that most of the (mechanisation) work falls within the province of technologists and managerial experts. The library profession can only state the requirements and indicate the areas where mechanisation will prove useful and also harmless [13]. Whereas modern librarians wanted to multitask as technologists and managerial experts, but that multitasking should not be at the cost of sacrificing librarian skills. The information specialist - the person who creates classifications, designs metadata protocols, crafts search capabilities for information system users, designs systems specifically for information retrieval - that person has an entirely different expertise than either the content expert or the programmer [10].

4. CONCLUSION

An information scientist of repute appreciated that Ranganathan is to library science what Einstein is to physics [11]. Librarians, computer scientists, and managers once lived in quite separate communities, each with its own terminology and often unaware that they addressed problems that looked different but were, in fact, substantially similar [7]. Let us hope that interactive research in these different areas would lead to effective analysis and efficient synthesis of ideas and evolving fully functional digital libraries satisfying 'user is the king' motive of Ranganathan's work. The three focus areas may create a professional role for librarians in the digital setup and work of library professionals indirectly open up products and processes of user friendly and user relevant information systems.

REFERENCES

1. Ranganathan, S R, Prolegomena to library classification, Bangalore: Sarada Ranganathan Endowment for Library Science, Chapter XA, 1967.
2. Ranganathan, S R, The Five Laws of Library Science, Bangalore: Sarada Ranganathan Endowment for Library Science, Ed. 2, Rep. 1988, pp. 352-353.
3. DLI Vision, dli.iiit.ac.in/vision.html
4. Op. Cit 2, p. 374.
5. Cloonan, Michèle V. and Dove, John G., Ranganathan Online, Do digital libraries violate the Third Law?, Library Journal, 4/1/2005, http://www.libraryjournal.com/article/CA512179.html

6. Denton, William. "Putting Facets on the Web: An Annotated Bibliography" Oct. 2003. *http://www.miskatonic.org/library/facet-biblio.html*

7. Gnoli, Claudio, Is there a role for traditional knowledge organization systems in the Digital Age?, http://eprints.rclis.org/archive/00001415/01/kos-role.htm

8. Denton, William. "How to Make a Faceted Classification and Put It On the Web" Nov. 2003, http://www.miskatonic.org/library/facet-web-howto.html

9. Glassel, Aimee, Was Ranganathan a Yahoo!?, March 1998, http://scout.wisc.edu/Projects/PastProjects/toolkit/enduser/archive/1998/euc-9803.html

10. Bates, Marcia J. After the Dot-Bomb: Getting Information Retrieval Right This Time, 2002, http://www.hastingsresearch.com/net/08-net-information-retrieval.shtml

11. Garfield, E, A Tribute to S. R. Ranganathan, the Father of Indian Library Science. Part 2. Contribution to Indian and International Library Science, Essays of an Information Scientist, Vol. 7, pp. 45-49, 1984.

12. Devadason, Francis. J. et al., Faceted Indexing Based System for Organizing and Accessing Internet Resources, http://www.geocities.com/devadason.geo/FactDSIS.pdf

13. Op. Cit 2, Ranganathan, p. 378.

10

PROFESSOR P N KAULA

1. INTRODUCTION

Prof. Kaula was no doubt the greatest library professional in the country after Dr. Ranganathan. He has achieved this unique position through sheer hard work, determination and perseverance. To him libraries, librarianship and information science were the be all and end all of life. An erudite scholar, expert teacher, able researcher, effective guide, meticulous editor, concerned activist and library advocate; the roles played by Prof. Kaula over his five decade old professional career are many [1, 2]. He lead a life which illustrates what is good and worth emulating in Indian librarianship.

2. ALWAYS SPOKE HIS MIND

In an interaction during one seminar, one person from the audience stood up and spoke with conviction about what should be done in respect of Ranganathan's Colon Classification scheme. He appeared as a person with pragmatic ideas to develop and popularize the classification scheme of the great Indian master. This episode revealed one of the main virtues of the man who is regarded as the true disciple of Ranganathan; uprightness and fearlessness to speak his mind. He has a massive fan following due to his words and actions. But he was not a man of the masses like present day politicians.

3. MOTIVATOR TO THE ROOT

In one of the interviews in a famous Central Government Institution, I had the good fortune to face Prof. Kaula in 1996. He was very encouraging in posing questions and eliciting replies. He made the candidates feel at home through out the interview process by cracking jokes and making comments in lighter vein. He has imbibed the qualities of a concerned teacher who places many leads in the question so that even an average student should be able to answer at least some points related to the question. While walking out of the interview room, I heard him his appreciative comments to other members of the Board in his typical roaring voice. Though not selected for the job, such a comment of him acted as a great motivator in all professional travails thereafter. As a great teacher, perhaps he might have known how such appreciation from peers rewards students/juniors. It is quite normal and natural for him to enquire about personal problems especially in regard to job and higher studies. The constant reminders he used to send regarding completion of Ph.D. which was one of the prime movers in my case where the work was delayed due to official and family pressures.

4. EDITOR PAR EXCELLENCE

My first paper in a journal has been published in Prof. Kaula's journal, Herald of Library Science. After sending the manuscript, I was waiting for a communication for its revision or rejection. Seeing the paper published in Herald, I felt elated because my paper has been examined thoroughly and passed successfully through his careful eyes. Who knows how many young authors has he motivated in this manner? Though a multifaceted personality, perhaps the biggest contribution he has made to the profession is the nurturing provided to two journals 'Herald of Library Science' (quarterly in the 47th year of publication) and 'International Information Communication and Education' (INICAE) (biannual in the 27th year of publication), both covered in international indexing and abstracting sources such as LISA strived hard to present the current status of research and academics in library science, information science and allied fields in India and developing world to a wider international audience. He joked once that his family used to comment the twin journals as his children as he spend more time on them. The key feature of these journals was not only the research papers (few of them even from foreign countries, developing countries in particular) but the news and notes section the Editor so meticulously prepared. He used to receive many journals on exchange against his journals and as a hardworking person dedicated to the discipline of library science, he curiously reads most of them and prepares notes out of them and shared it with professionals in a digest form through his journals. We may not appreciate the importance of this feature in the post Internet era where information concerning anything is accessible at the touch of a button. When he started 'notes and news', information was not so forthcoming and hence it acted as a major source of meeting 'current approach' of the information needs of many professionals. He was very pluralistic and accommodative while accepting papers solely judged by quality and no other extraneous considerations. He practiced the high ideals of 'nishkama karma' in his conduct as an editor of professional journals and always practiced what he preached. The subject matter of papers published in these journals is so varied, has authors young and old; experienced as well as fresh; publishes papers from developed as well as developing countries and to a large extent free from any editorial bias.

5. TEACHER OF TEACHERS

Prof. Kaula endeared himself to the students through sheer motivation and maintained a high standard of discipline and insistence on library hours and tutorials. May be due to the peculiarities of students taking up library courses and the entrants being a mix of Arts, Science and other streams, he might have thought about enforcing a strict regime.

In a conference in 2002 more on IT aspects with new generation of library professionals as most of the participants to discuss and debate about the latest technology applications in libraries, his keynote lecture on 'Relevance of Ranganathan' was kept as a connection of the past with the present and future. Prof. Kaula justified his position in the profession by enthralling the audience with a thought provoking lecture on the applicability of Ranganathan's research to solve some of the problems of organizing and retrieving e-information also. His spellbound lecture was interspersed with anecdotes of his interaction with the great master and the hall was packed with most of the conference attendees.

6. BREATHED AND LIVED LIBRARY SCIENCE

Emilia Curras mentioned that even on a visit to Spain where other international scholars used to take time out to visit at least places of interest for sight seeing, Prof. Kaula was so immersed in his academic activities of teaching, research and writing [3]. He led a busy life in the profession as a teacher, researcher, expert, editor, activist and many other roles for the welfare and improvement of libraries and its professionals. In short he spent an active professional life of more than 5 decades as a role model for professionals.

7. TREATED EVERYONE AS EQUAL

Perhaps his Kashmiri upbringing and the diverse experience he gained during studies and work in different parts of the country made him a true cosmopolitan. He never favoured a particular region, religion, or language and treated everyone as equal. He had the vastness to talk to a senior professional and student of library science in their different wavelengths as he was an effective communicator.

8. MOST HUMBLE

In a conference while passing few of the techno savvy professionals, he commented 'I have no role among the technology experts'. With so many achievements in different and diverse spheres of professional activity, he always remained humble in his conduct. Perhaps he was the last of the Gandhians in Library Science for that matter.

9. LETTERS

With phone, email, mobile and SMS emerging as new modes of communication, we hardly write letters these days and perhaps as a person of the last generations, Prof. Kaula developed a habit to communicate as far as possible with short and to the point letters. Many professionals are fortunate to receive inspiring letters from him. He used to be precise and to the point in his letters, some handwritten, some typed, and some in post cards. One of the concerns of his letters is about ensuring subscription to journals edited by him in the libraries. He used to read papers for publication meticulously and then replied the authors about his comments and assessment of the paper. He had no qualms in accepting good points made by junior professionals. He himself wrote in one letter which underlines his habit of wiring letters as "I always reply back to the letters received. There may be some delay but I must answer back. That is my habit". Sometimes when an author reports about non-receipt of the author copy of the journal, he immediately replies seeking the residential address of the author and ensuring despatch of an alternate copy of the journal. One letter relates to his assessment of a paper published in a journal not edited by him. This shows his professionalism. How many of the senior professionals think of writing to a junior author about a paper? In a letter in 2004, he highlights his undying spirit for work "My health has also entered into a period of weakness and other problems. God knows if I can continue with the work of the journals... I will go on with the work till I am unable to do." In his counsel to a young professional, he wrote "Please never rest on and continue your work in all circumstances. Work has also its own reward." No wonder many professionals cherish these inspiring and educative letters as souvenirs. They continue to rightly guide professionals, young and old in the professional path ahead.

10. CONTRIBUTIONS

Prof. Kaula has authored/edited 60 plus books/ Monographs, 6 Professional Journals (Founder-Editor) and over 400 scholarly papers, over 400 reviews, 43 bibliographies and 6000 digests and notes [4]. An analysis of his 100 papers covered in LISA is attempted here and in the Table below. Out of which, 87 papers (87%) were published in Herald of Library Science, 5 papers (5%) in INICAE, 2 papers each in 'International Classification' and 'International Forum on Information and Documentation' and one paper each in Granthana, Journal of Library and Information Science (India), Lucknow Librarian and Unesco Bulletin for Libraries. Only three papers were coauthored whereas the remaining 97 papers were written alone. These 100 papers account for 619 pages which lead to an average of 6 pages per paper which tells about his efficiency in summarizing relevant points regarding a topic in few pages with enhanced readability. His style was to present a topic to the layman so that both experts and beginners take advantage of his writings. One paper each was published in 1974, 1992, 1994, 1995, 1996, 1997, 2002 and 2006. Two papers each were published in 1973, 1975, 1978, 1985, 1987, 1998, 1999 and 2000 while three papers each were published in 1977, 1988, 1990, 1991, 1993 and 2001. Four papers each were published in 1971, 1976, 1979 and 1984. During the years 1969, 1972, 1980, 1981, 1983 and 1989 five papers each were published. The maximum number of 6 papers was published in 1970 and 1982. As far as the subject coverage is concerned, crucial topics of more concern to him are librarianship (15%), public libraries (13%), library science education (10%), technical services (9%, four papers each on cataloging and classification and one on indexing), libraries (7%), user services (6%) and report of conferences/seminars attended (5%). There are four papers each on S R Ranganathan, education, information work and library staff and three papers on national libraries. Nine subjects have two papers each covering Andhra Pradesh, Bibliometrics, college libraries, Government department libraries, library information technology, library legislation, library policies, professional/staff salaries and school libraries. There are 58 other subjects having one paper each.

Table: Prof. Kaula's papers from LISA

No.	Subject	Journal	Year	Pages	Remarks
1	Public libraries	Herald	2006	8	
2	National Library	Herald	2002	11	
3	Social science information	INICAE	2001	9	
4	Library information technology	Herald	2001	4	
5	Librarianship-Punjab	Herald	2001	7	
6	Public libraries	Herald	2000	7	
7	Academic libraries	Herald	2000	9	
8	Health care	INICAE	1999	10	
9	Adult education, public libraries	Herald	1999	8	

10	National Book Museum	INICAE	1998	9	
11	Preservation, digitization	INICAE	1998	2	
12	Library policies, cost benefit analysis	Herald	1997	10	
13	Public libraries, networks	Herald	1996	7	
14	College libraries, Public libraries, Haryana	Herald	1995	6	
15	Library information technology	Herald	1994	4	
16	LIS education	INICAE	1993	10	
17	Government department libraries	Herald	1993	11	
18	Rangnathan, S R	Herald	1993	19	
19	Rangnathan, S R	JLIS, India	1992	16	JLIS, India-Journal of Library and Information Science
20	User services, Gatekeepers	IFID	1991	6	IFID-International Forum on Information and Documentation
21	Conference Report	Herald	1991	8	
22	School libraries, Public libraries	Granthana	1991	10	
23	Library staff, Women	Herald	1990	8	
24	Librarianship	Herald	1990	12	
25	Librarianship, Special libraries	Herald	1990	13	
26	Democracy, Libraries	Herald	1989	4	
27	School libraries	Herald	1989	2	
28	Area studies, library materials	Herald	1989	6	
29	Public libraries, Jammu and Kashmir	Herald	1989	6	
30	Technical services, Periodicals	Herald	1989	7	
31	LIS education	Herald	1988	8	
32	Libraries, education	Herald	1988	7	

33	Education policy, Library service, Engineering education	Herald	1988	7	
34	LIS Education, Universe of knowledge	Herald	1987	6	
35	Library staff, Salaries	Herald	1987	6	
36	Librarianship, Library staff	Herald	1985	5	
37	National Policies, Library and information services	Herald	1985	5	
38	User services, Information work	IFID	1984	5	
39	Bibliometrics, Technical services, cataloguing	Herald	1984	13	
40	Technical services, Classification	Herald	1984	15	
41	Librarianship	Herald	1984	4	
42	Public libraries, Orissa	LL	1983	7	LL- Lucknow Librarian
43	Public libraries, literacy	Herald	1983	2	
44	Profession, Librarianship	Herald	1983	3	
45	College libraries	Herald	1983	11	
46	User services, Information work	Herald	1983	5	
47	LIS education	Herald	1982	7	
48	Shera, J H	Herald	1982	2	
49	User services, Information work	Herald	1982	5	
50	Librarianship	Herald	1982	4	
51	Librarianship, Andhra Pradesh	Herald	1982	4	
52	Technical services, classification	Herald	1982	5	
53	National libraries, India	Herald	1981	11	
54	Librarianship	Herald	1981	8	
55	Librarianship, West Germany	Herald	1981	20	
56	Technical services, classification	IC	1981	5	IC- International Classification
57	Librarianship, Hungary	Herald	1981	5	
58	Citation analysis, Bibliometrics, Social sciences	Herald	1980	10	Co-author with Singh, S N
59	Indian Ocean area, User services, Information work	Herald	1980	15	

60	Librarianship, Conference report	Herald	1980	5	Co-author with Singh, S N
61	Technical services, Classification Canons	IC	1980	8	
62	Public libraries, Andhra Pradesh	Herald	1980	11	
63	Librarianship, Library Day	Herald	1979	4	
64	Technical services, cataloguing	Herald	1979	14	Co-author with Singh, S N
65	LIS Education, Continuing education	Herald	1979	7	
66	Information science, User services	Herald	1979	10	
67	IFLA, Conference report	Herald	1978	11	
68	LIS education	Herald	1978	7	
69	Library legislation, UK	Herald	1977	12	
70	Libraries, India	Herald	1977	10	
71	Technical services, cataloguing, Urdu	Herald	1977	7	
72	Dewey M	Herald	1976	12	
73	Bhatia S R	Herald	1976	4	
74	Bashiruddin S	Herald	1976	4	
75	National libraries, Japan	Herald	1976	6	
76	Public libraries, Mahatma Gandhi	Herald	1975	4	
77	Librarianship, East Germany	Herald	1975	20	
78	LIS education	Herald	1974	4	
79	Ranganathan S R	Herald	1973	20	
80	Librarianship	Herald	1973	9	
81	Public libraries, Uttar Pradesh	Herald	1972	9	
82	Ranganathan S R	Herald	1972	3	
83	Library legislation	Herald	1972	3	
84	Public libraries	Herald	1972	3	
85	Libraries, Israel	Herald	1972	8	
86	Conference report	Herald	1971	13	

87	LIS education	Herald	1971		
88	Technical services, cataloguing	Herald	1971	4	
89	Bodleian Library, James Thomas	Herald	1971	2	
90	Library associations, India	UBL	1970	7	UBL-Unesco Bulletin for Libraries
91	LIS education, Canada	Herald	1970	5	
92	Chain indexing	Herald	1970	8	
93	William Ewart	Herald	1970	5	
94	Government department libraries, Library staff, Salaries	Herald	1970	20	
95	LIS education	Herald	1970	5	
96	Colon Classification, Notation	Herald	1969	3	
97	National institutions, India, libraries	Herald	1969	6	
98	Religious libraries, Vatican Library	Herald	1969	4	
99	Education, libraries	Herald	1969	7	
100	Education, libraries, seminar report	Herald	1969	11	

11. CRITICS GALORE

It is common for a successful person to attract critics and criticism. Like Dr. Ranganathan, Prof. Kaula also has adversaries. He was a pioneering figure and towering personality among library activists of his time and hence got involved in many national and international bodies. This coupled with two strong journals under his command put him in better visibility than many of his contemporaries. His upright nature of calling a spade a spade also antagonized many. There were also criticisms about him using journals for his own publicity. Such critics always forget the fact that the same journals also projected the achievements of many professionals in different ways.

12 GIVE ALL AND TAKE NOTHING

It was Prof. Kaula's uniqueness that he could give all but take back nothing. For him guiding and directing a student in the right path of professionalism and ensuring the student's conduct so was the only 'gurudakshina' he cherished.

13. CONCLUSION

Prof. Kaula lived a life rich in legacy and professionalism. His heroisms continue to inspire professionals for many years to come. Some other professional journals floated by peers in many fields failed into oblivion at a later stage due to the absence of an institutional mechanism to sustain such journals. The best tribute we can pay to him is by creating some sustaining mechanism so that the two journals, his brainchildren, continue to appear in print revealing the latest and best in Indian library research. He once remarked librarianship as an enigma infested profession and his successful life and fruitful work over the years was nothing but as a herald to interpret its nuances thereby guiding today's and tomorrow's professionals.

REFERENCES

1. 6 articles and 1 poem in celebration of the 61st birthday of Prof. P N Kaula, Herald of Library Science, 26 (3-4), July October 1987, pp. 221-247.
2. March of library science: Kaula Festschrift, Delhi, Vikas Publishing House Pvt Ltd., 1979, 626 p.
3. Curras, Emilia, In honour of Professor Kaula: Impact of his work in Spain, Herald of Library Science, 32 (3-4), July-October 1993, pp. 213-217.
4. Prof Kaula Endowment for Library and Information Science, http://www.kaulaendowment.org/

11

STOCK VERIFICATION

1. INTRODUCTION

A senior professor in a premier academic institution got so agitated when a proposal was brought by librarian in the Library Committee to increase the fine charged for overdue books and cost realization of lost books from teachers. His argument ran on these lines: 'I operate multi crore projects where instruments and equipments worth crores and consumables worth lakhs were spent for research. Nobody has so far questioned me or charged fines when these get obsolete or damaged whereas if I issue a book of few hundreds of rupees and I have to account for it till my retirement'. This aberration in rules has come up due to the difference in which equipments, consumables and library books are treated by the Government. The General Financial Rules (GFR), 2005, Government of India defines in its 'Rule 136' the term 'goods' as "all articles, material, commodities, livestock, furniture, fixtures, raw material, spares, instruments, machinery, equipment, industrial plant etc. purchased or otherwise acquired for the use of Government but excludes books, publications, periodicals, etc. for a library" [1]. In no other area of loss like that of minor equipment and consumable in any organisation so much of fuss about responsibility of loss arises as it happens in loss of library documents [2].

All those items regarded as goods have a certain lifetime and if the goods are put to good use for a certain period, the purpose of it is regarded as served. However this is not the case with library books which are considered as items of eternal value and hence they are to be preserved for posterity. It is true that some books have eternal value as far as subject matter is concerned whereas many books, not to mention disciplines like science and technology, even in humanities and social sciences get obsolete in a short span of time. Also the paper and print quality of many of the books printed in developing countries like ours get worn out so fast in personal collections also, let alone the multiple uses in a library severely impacting their lifespan. Added to this is the responsibility assigned to librarian and library staff as custodians of these materials and in many institutions, they are being victimised for any loss (beyond the permissible limit) which in all probability takes a heavy toll on our libraries and their services. This acts like a vicious circle that lack of services lead to mutilations and theft by users and responsibility on staff for mutilation/theft further derailing quality and range of access and services.

2. REVIEW OF EARLIER STUDIES

Senapati discusses the importance of stock verification and shelf rectification [3]. Dhiman highlights the different problems of stock verification of electronic publications with special reference to CD-ROMs [4]. Moorthy raises pertinent additional points [5] not discussed by Dhiman on software locking in the case of CD-ROM databases, and subscriptions to online publications. Kumbar presents report of a survey on stock verification in college libraries in Shimoga City, Karnataka using questionnaires sent to 17 college libraries and information taken from the responses of 15. 13 of these colleges reported about losses of books in varying numbers and proposes student counselling as the most effective long term method of decreasing book theft [6]. Sridhar highlights the norms and procedures of stock verification for Government of India libraries and various methods of physical verification [2].

3. STATUS IN OTHER COUNTRIES

As per the information available from a reputed University Library, there is no national policy in U. K. which obliges university or public libraries to formally account for stolen or missing books. Though the University auditors can inspect library expenditure at any time, but that audit trail would not be complete where a book has subsequently been withdrawn from stock for any reason, including theft. Libraries do carry out "stock check" for heavily used collections, mainly so that the catalogue remains up to date and for purchasing required replacement copies. The procedure turned out to be very time consuming and error prone for less heavily used research collections and hence extensive checks for a particular item would be made if any customer reports about a missing item leading to that item being found, replaced, or withdrawn. A mail to the JISCMAIL listserv to collect more details about how other Universities in U. K. handle this crucial issue could not gather response from any other University/Institution.

Attempts to gather information from other countries with exceptional library facilities also failed perhaps due to differing perception of library administrators towards library operations. In a search in LISA for stock verification, stock checking and stock counting, 68 references were found out of which 26 pertain to studies by authors from India.

4. ADDRESSING MISSING/MUTILATED COLLECTION

4.1. Lack of Training in Responsible Library Use

We have comparatively better services in university and research libraries due to the large collection in these institutions cushioning off the 0.5% ceiling imposed by GFR making library staff to courageously practice open access apart from providing useful services to readers. This is not the case with libraries with smaller collection like those in schools and colleges. Many school libraries operate with a teacher in-charge who never issue out books or practice it as a ritual once in a while. In many colleges due to the punitive clauses on account of loss, librarians practice closed access or keep the library out of bounds for the large gamut of student users.

Apart from missing books, another problem libraries have to deal with is the tearing of pages from books and journals. One often wonders why this is happening in the best of libraries with liberal provisions for issuing out collection or/and photocopying. Perhaps the seeds of these are to be found in the socio cultural features of citizens. Most of the students have very limited access to libraries in schools and colleges and many get exposed to first class library facilities in the University/research libraries. Students not trained in library centred education in the schools and colleges are later not able to take advantage of the collection and services available in university libraries; this may be one of the reasons for the poor use of some of the best such libraries. Since they are not trained in responsible use right from the beginning, at least some users are prone to misusing the facilities.

Apart from intensifying vigilance, extended library hours during examination time, liberal or subsidised xerox service and liberal lending of books marked 'not to be issued' [2] help to reduce theft/mutilation. Librarians should not forget that one of the reasons for mutilation/theft in many libraries is the stringent user-unfriendly policies and practices. The proud reference collection acquired in a premier university library were mutilated by student users as a result of restriction on library photocopying (of only 20 pages can be requested by a user and very limited number of requests accepted in a day) further with no policy for issuing reference book even for a short duration. To save libraries of higher education and research from this menace, the best way to address this issue is by extending user-friendly library rules and instilling the responsible use behaviour right from the school level with maturing these trends in the college level too. In an academic institution, sometimes the teachers refer to a particular book and there is a fight among students to get access to the same and some students feel it a matter of happiness to hide/steal that book so that fellow students do not get access to the same. Sridhar rightly said a negligible number of perverted, possessive, habituated persons responsible for loss and mutilation is likely to continue in spite of liberalised services and strict vigilance [2].

4.2. Absence of Proper Security Systems

Many libraries are not equipped with automated security systems like CCTV and RFID, so that the responsibility of ensuring the security and safety of collection rests with limited number of staff members who are often overburdened with routine library operations and the compulsion to perform extra duties during lunch break and night. With many adolescent users thronging the stack rooms and other service areas of a library, it is difficult to ensure proper vigil even for the most alert staff. The vigil by library personnel must be supplemented with proper and latest technology solutions to discourage pilferage and mutilation of the library collection. Technology solutions often act as a better deterrent and this coupled with alertness of staff can work wonders on the security front in a library where users of different character traits and social/behavioural/cultural attitudes visit regularly.

4.3. Need for Secure Circulation Systems

The libraries should also have a fool proof circulation system to properly account for books and other reading materials issued out for use by the clients. In libraries with computer savvy users, it is not appropriate to disregard manual checks in computerized circulation system. It is always ideal to generate issue slips in triplicate through computer and obtain the signature of the patron in these slips. Apart from maintaining the master slip at the issue counter which may be tallied with the slips collected from users at the security counter. One copy of the receipt for the patron may also alert the user about the books issued from the library and their due date for return. Other computer network security options like issue-return module only accessible in certain machines of the library at the circulation counter, generating random passwords for circulation staff, barcode input of passwords for circulation staff etc., may also be adopted to eliminate any cases of password guessing and possible trespass into library circulation system.

5. COLLECTION MANAGEMENT ISSUES

5.1. Cost of Library Collection

Rules and regulations regarding missing/mutilated collection only attributes to the quantitative aspects of the collection disregarding its qualitative aspects. What will happen if few pages are missing from an out of print book which is heavily used in the institution? If that is the only copy available in the institution or country, how to take care of satisfying the urges of interested users? A book/journal purchased in the library has not only its purchase cost but there are certain additional hidden costs too. Some of these include the cost of cataloguing, classifying and maintaining the item by spending staff salaries and other maintenance costs. If we take into account these additional costs, the cost of a book/journal is much more than its purchase cost. Considering the returns brought to the Institution and country as a result of the productive use of library collection, one can better evaluate the impact of the missing and mutilated collection in the ongoing academic and research exercise. Some attempts at mutilation/theft by few elements in the user community may be creating an irreparable loss to the whole academic community in many cases.

5.2. Cost Recovery

Libraries which lent out collection to users are prone to certain cases of users misplacing or losing the books. To discourage these cases, libraries normally adopt clauses like the defaulter paying the current price of the book plus a percentage of the processing charges or if the book is not available currently the old price plus penalty charges. Libraries encourage users to replace the current edition of the book to ensure the availability of the title in the collection. The fines collected for loss of books get deposited in the Institution's Account and never come back to library for refurbishing the collection. In some cases, the book lost may also be an out of print title making its purchase practically impossible. With economical editions of many foreign publishers started in the country, sometimes librarians may find it difficult to convince academic users about not accepting a local edition in lieu of the original edition lost considering the better quality of paper, printing and binding of that edition. They may argue about the content being same or current than the lost copy. Libraries and librarians should frame proper clauses in rules regarding replacement of lost book to counter such trends, which in the long run may replace original editions of libraries with reprints of inferior quality editions produced for personal use.

There may be provision in the acquisition rules to procure new copies of those books available for purchase for which prices are recovered. Normally the money deposited by users goes into some other budget head of the Institution making it not available for reuse by the library. There are also obstacles in procuring new copies without proper recommendations for purchase from users.

5.3. Weeding and Remote Stacking

Weeding is a problem with many libraries due to rules not permitting the same. American Center and British Libraries demonstrated in the country how a carefully maintained active collection by weeding out unwanted as well as less used ones periodically improves the overall functioning and serviceability of the library. Library professionals know the difficulties of maintaining active collection with less/never used titles in the same stack area creating many practical problems in stack maintenance. The less used books in the stacks encourage users who want to misplace and hide useful books in such areas. Public funded libraries have stricter rules for weeding and hence librarians fear to tread on that path often leaving the library with many older and less used books. Some librarians tried to get over this problem by identifying less used titles from the active collection and keeping them in a remote stack. Though libraries did it by considering circulation statistics and assessing books normally taken out for reading in the stack rooms by users, senior users have academic ways of explaining why some books used less are of more academic worth. Sometimes these remote stacks are not accessible all times like normal stacks. This and users interest to have all their books of interest in one place make it practically difficult for libraries to proceed with remote stacking of less used collection. Some libraries involved users to identify the titles of less interest without much success. Though difficult to arrive at a consensus by library professionals, it is advisable to have a very active stack area for more current and frequently used titles leaving the less used as well as old books to a separate area, which should be done only after convincing the users and library committee of the benefits of such a step. Provision may also be made at the same time for not denying any user access to the less used books in the remote stacks upholding the spirit of five laws of library science.

6. STOCK VERIFICATION

6.1. Why physical verification?

Many institutions with good libraries in the country are under the aegis of the Government and they have to follow the General Financial Rules (GFR) for their operations. The GFR 'Rule 194' prescribes about physical verification of library books:

- Complete physical verification of books should be done every year in case of libraries having not more than twenty thousand volumes.
- For libraries having more than twenty thousand volumes and up to fifty thousand volumes, such verification should be done at least once in three years.
- Sample physical verification at intervals of not more than three years should be done in case of libraries having more than fifty thousand volumes. In case any sample verification reveals unusual or unreasonable shortages, complete verification shall be done.

So with the help of this rule, Librarian can identify the frequency and mode for conducting stock verification based on the size of library collection. For smaller libraries, it is less cumbersome and beneficial from service point of view to carry out periodic stock checks thereby ensuring that the catalogue information comply with actual holdings. There may be queries from the Internal or/and External Audits in case of Government Institutions every year about stock verification, though Auditors are very well aware of the concerned GFR norms. As a result of this, sometimes Librarians have to justify about delay or postponement of stock verification.

6.2. Options for Stock Verification

Prasad suggests different methods for stock verification using shelf lists, accession register or accession number on sheets [8]. These methods are essentially manual systems leading to time delays and prone to human errors. Chandel and Walia present a computer assisted stock verification system which proved to be most advantageous and cost effective in comparison with other methods [7].

With library automation systems and barcoding gaining more prominence, libraries can read the barcode data of books using a barcode data collector terminal thus verifying easily the books present in the stacks. This data together with library issue and bindery records when matched with library collection records in the automation system would give the accession number of missing books. If library automation packages do not provide options for collection verification, library has to use standalone programs to print the accession numbers missing in the two lists. This process becomes much faster with RFID systems but unfortunately very few libraries have such systems presently in the country.

6.3. Who will conduct Stock Verification?

The onus on stock verification is put on library staff by majority of the Institutions which appears to be a wrong practice. It is not advisable to hand over the task of verifying the collection to the same persons who manage it, whatsoever one talk about professionalism and professional roles. Though some library professionals may get leave/ honorarium to shoulder this task, it is better to divest this task from library staff already overburdened with other tasks. Some institutions assigned this task to a committee of users without much success.

This activity may ideally be assigned to a professional consulting firm with a clearly defined job contract detailing the activities to be performed, duration of the job, work timings on weekdays and weekends, profiles of persons engaged with their identity proof, reports to be submitted, charges with breakup in different heads. It is difficult to find agencies and consultants in an organized fashion in many parts of the county though one could find few firms experienced in this activity in major cities. Also the demand is very short for many players to sustain in this activity. Once there is a demand for periodic verification from major libraries, there may be no dearth of agencies or consultants interested in this activity. This may also offer some incentive to retired professionals and young professionals on the look out for temporary jobs. Library associations, library networks, library automation firms, agencies engaged in retro-conversion also may be lured to offer consultancy in this area.

6.4. Permissible loss

The GFR Rule 194 again identifies what is a permissible loss in the context of library:

- Loss of five volumes per one thousand volumes of books issued/consulted in a year may be taken as reasonable provided such losses are not attributable to dishonesty or negligence.
- However, loss of a book of a value exceeding Rs. 1,000/- (Rupees One thousand only) and rare books irrespective of value shall invariably be investigated and appropriate action taken.

The first statement suggests that 0.5% of losses as reasonable provided it is not on account of dishonesty or negligence of library staff. Thus stock verification is "covertly viewed as a tool to punish librarians" [2]. Library staff also comes from the society and hence we can only expect honesty and attention in the case of library staff as that for staff working in other departments and offices of the Institution. Work related weathering and frustration are part of personnel working in library like those posted in other departments of any institution. There are several occupations where persons are entrusted with responsibilities and they were not punished or victimized when something goes wrong or some untoward incident happens. Are we going to recover the cost of a failed satellite from the salary of scientists and engineers involved in its development? We have not heard about many cases of recovering the cost of a faulty flyover from the Engineers and contractors involved in its construction? The library personnel make every attempt to minimize the losses due to theft and mutilation but penalizing them for any determined effort by suspicious elements may have serious bearing on the library's overall services.

Fixing a value of Rs. 1000 is very nominal as production costs have substantially increased the cost of books printed in the country itself. Same is the case for books published abroad with price in foreign currencies and their spiraling exchange rates which form a major portion of the collection of many academic and research libraries in the country. Considering the average price of a foreign book purchased in a library, this may be enhanced to at least Rs. 10000 so that there is a purpose in investigation and follow up action in the case of significant losses. There may be provision also for raising this price on an annual basis reflecting the overall escalation in book prices.

7. LIBRARY SERVICE IS PRIME

7.1. Preservation Not Verification

The rules which put tough clauses on preventing missing of books unfortunately do not put the same emphasis on the preservation aspect of library collection. Many libraries receive very little amount for this crucial activity. Majority of the books printed in the country for obvious reasons to maintain low price are printed using poor quality paper making these unserviceable after few years of handling. This coupled with the severe weather conditions prevailing in the country with no provision for Air-conditioning in many libraries coupled with the continuous multiple use put these books, acquired with much effort on the part of faculty and library staff, faster to deterioration.

7.2. Effective Stacking

It is the duty of every library to maintain the stacks of the library as effective as possible to uphold the professional and service spirit enshrined in the five laws of library science. The books should be found in the appropriate location as provided by the catalogue search. In the earlier days, manual catalogue search using cards found it little cumbersome for a user to identify easily all the different facets of a topic whereas the details of titles matching a query are flashed immediately from OPAC making users more demanding for more titles of interest from stacks. So the stacks should be equipped to handle such increasing demand for relevant titles and hence care should be taken to ensure better stack rectification and stack and spine labeling to facilitate easier retrieval of titles on demand by users.

7.3. Guidance through Osmosis

Ranganathan propounded the law of osmosis to guide changing of classification and cataloguing for only heavily used collection [9]. This principle may also be extended to how the library may offer better services without resorting to frequent stock verification. Whenever a user reports about any book or other reading material not traceable, efforts must be made to trace it out. If that effort is not successful, a fresh copy of the same may be procured if available for purchase when the demand for the title justifies that or else source a copy through Inter Library Loan. There are cases that an item not be located at one time may reappear in the stacks at a later stage as users may sometimes misplace books in an open access library.

7.4. Not to abandon midway

Sometimes out of pressure, libraries venture into stock verification and abandon it midway when there is a change in the managerial setup which will do more harm than good. Once an exercise in stock verification was initiated, it should be taken to its logical conclusion by preparing the required reports and submit the same to the competent authority for follow up action so that the future verification exercise may not carry the burden of previous losses.

7.5. Elimination of Vindictive Clauses

One way for the libraries and librarians to willingly accept stock verification into the routine activities is by eliminating the vindictive clauses presently existing in rules and regulations concerning stock verification. Instead of blaming and penalizing library staff, this may be viewed as an operational and managerial activity undertaken to improve the overall serviceability of the library. Such a change in mindset may also overcome the present obstacles in following open access system and barrier free library services. This would also motivate the library professionals to ensure that stacks hold the stock reflected in the catalogue. They may also willingly and sincerely report any mutilation or theft occurred, if any, if the punitive clauses concerning stock verification are abolished.

8. ISSUES AND CHALLENGES

- Interference and concerted efforts from professionals, associations and serious users are required to get the prevalent rules for stock verification amended so that the service aspect of library may be put as prime rather than viewing the library as a stockpile.
- If abandoning the stock verification is difficult, then at least the punitive clauses against library professionals may be scrapped at the earliest so that the books kept out of bounds from users should be put to better use.
- We can not have better higher education libraries unless we have better libraries in schools and colleges and also public libraries to instill responsive use behaviour right from childhood.
- Users should be apprised of the copyright rules, the need to comply with copyright rules and the imporatance of honouring the intellectual property rights of authors. Subsequently, libraries at all levels should have liberal provision of document copying facilities. It is difficult to handle all the copying load on the library alone and hence ample provision may be made to clear the extra load through private operators in proximity.
- Libraries should practice user friendly rules for issuing out collection. There may be provision for issuing out reference collection and journal volumes on an hourly basis or for overnight use so that the urge to resort to mutilation could be curtailed.
- Indian editions of many foreign books at nominal cost have reduced mutilation of text books to a large extent. This has also made it possible for libraries to buy multiple copies of books to match user demand.
- Technology alone will not solve the problem of theft and mutilation. Sometimes users are more techno

savvy and they could break into the library circulation systems and modify transaction data. Thus libraries would also maintain minimum but essential records about issue records in print format of 'issue (acceptance) slips' to deter suspicious and adolescent users to tamper with library computer systems.

- Technologies like CCTV and security systems using electro magnetic and RFID technology would definitely act as a deterrent against mutilation/theft of the library collection. The feeling that someone with better attention span than a human is watching would dissuade many problematic elements from attempting to tamper or steal library books.
- Efficient management of book stacks would also eliminate causes of mutilation/theft. Separating out old and less used materials depending on the core and non-core areas of the institution to separate stacks or separate location provides a pruned active stack of more functional library collection. This eliminates to some extent surreptitious elements from taking advantage of less used areas of stacks as pockets for hiding/tampering books.
- The increasing emphasis put on electronic access in higher education and research libraries made it possible for books and journals to be accessed in electronic form from the websites of publishers and aggregators leaving mutilation/theft of resources a non-issue. However a whole set of new issues such as network security, complying with license rules without sacrificing the academic and research interests of users, and ensuring that only authorized users can access and use our cyber library gain more prominence in the emerging context.

9. CONCLUSION

Stock verification helps to reduce unnecessary escalation in book value of assets; replace relevant, useful and on demand documents; introduce new ways of stack arrangement, lending system and other procedures; users can browse the entire collection; review the precautionary measures in preventing loss and mutilation; identify and discard obsolete volumes; identify damaged documents for repair; keep shelf list and other records up-to-date; rearrangement and cleaning of stack; better acquaintance of collection and popular documents by library staff, etc. [2]. No rule of stock verification must hinder the service aspect of a library or cast aspersions on the behavioural attitudes and performance levels of library staff. The paw or teeth in stock verification norms may be clipped suitably to make the library experience of students in schools and colleges more pleasant. There must be some metrics to assess use of resources disregarding minor losses in a library by empowering users and staff. The increasing emphasis paid on electronic access in higher academic and research libraries would have to address larger issues of network security, complying with license rules without disregarding academic and research interests of users and ensuring that only authorized users access our cyber library. The modern librarian is more aware of his/her limitations with respect to technology skills and availability, limited budgets and unlimited resources, abundant user requirements and unlimited user expectations. S/he would be more than willing to enhance usage of resources by risking the restrictions in the 'rule book' for making the user's information experience very richer. It is time for Government and Institutional heads to suitably make amends in the stock verification rules without jeopardizing the service ideals of an important service unit like library without victimizing the library staff. Professional accountability should not be addressed by enforcing tougher clauses for victimization but by empowering profession and professionals in a democratic atmosphere with full freedom so that library profession should deliver better results.

REFERENCES

1. General Financial Rules, 2005, Government of India, Ministry of Finance, Department of Expenditure, http://finmin.nic.in/the_ministry/dept_expenditure/GFRS/GFR2005.pdf
2. Sridhar, M. S. Library stock verification: a ritual and an occupational hazard, IASLIC Bulletin, 36(3), 1991, pp. 103-110.
3. Senapati, S K, Physical verification of library: some basic issues, Herald of Library Science; 40 (1-2) Jan-Apr 2001, pp. 94-96.
4. Dhiman, A K, Stock verification: some problems of electronic publications, DESIDOC Bulletin of Information Technology; 20 (6) Nov 2000, pp. 3-5.
5. Moorthy, A L, Stock verification of electronic publications: a rejoinder, DESIDOC Bulletin of Information Technology; 20 (6) Nov 2000, pp. 7-8.
6. Kumbar, M, Stock verification and loss of books in college libraries: a survey, SRELS Journal of Information Management; 37 (3) Sep 2000, pp. 189-197.
7. Chandel, A S; Walia, R K, Computer-assisted stock-verification system, Libri; 43 (2) Apr-Jun 93, pp. 108-122.
8. Prasad, B. K. Stock Verification, Loss of Books and Weeding, Ch. 11 in Encyclopaedia of Teaching of Library Science, New Delhi, Anmol, 2003, pp. 275-283.
9. Ranganathan, S R, Prolegomena to Library Classification, Sarada Ranganathan Endowment for Library Science, Bangalore, 3rd ed., 1994 reprint, pp. 136-139.

12

Sixth Pay Commission

1. INTRODUCTION

The successive pay commissions and expert committees (with a biased representation of teachers) somehow tried to undermine the working library professionals. This is evident in the way working professionals and teachers progress in any organisation in the country. The most appalling fact is that all this is done after persons with same qualifications are recruited in the entry level positions of Asst. Librarian/Lecturer and in the further career, both streams trying to meet the dual objectives of information support for teaching, learning and research. The UGC has issued on 30th June 2010 'Regulations on Minimum Qualifications for Appointment of Teachers and other Academic Staff in Universities and Colleges and Measures for the Maintenance of Standards in Higher Education 2010' [1]. The regulations shall be applicable to teachers and other equivalent cadres of Library and Physical Education in all the Central Universities and Colleges there-under and the Institutions Deemed to be Universities whose maintenance expenditure is met by the UGC. More or less, the state universities are also going to follow these recommendations to claim UGC grants. These Regulations came after another document [2], both are supposed to be based, rather an implementation note, on the Report of the UGC Pay Review Committee (PRC). A quick perusal of these documents shows that some recommendations of the PRC were ignored in the Regulations.

All the library cadres may have suffered some discrimination or other with respective cadre of teachers. It is not clear whether all University Librarians were fixed at Rs. 43000 like directly recruited Professors. Ten percent of Professors shall be with AGP of 12000 selected from Professors with 10 years of service subject to performance evaluation by an expert committee which appears to be not extended to Librarians. Similarly only affected University Assistant Librarians /College Librarians can throw more light on anomalies in their career advancement or direct recruitment with respect to equivalent cadres of teachers. The Regulations have come as a big hit to the Deputy Librarians who have lost their parity with teachers as well as chances of CAS even after obtaining positive recommendation from the PRC.

2. COVERAGE OF LIBRARIANS AND PHYSICAL EDUCATORS

Out of 130 pages [1], let us look at the coverage given to each of these categories. The minimum qualifications for direct recruitment to Librarian categories are presented in pages 29-30 and the same for Physical Education Cadres in pages 30-32. The stages of promotion under the Career Advancement Scheme (CAS) for Assistant Librarians etc. are presented on pages 45-47. Pay Scales and CAS Regulations for Librarians etc. are discussed in pages 66-70. Incentives for Ph.D./M.Phil. and other higher qualifications for librarian and physical educations cadres are highlighted in pages 72-73. Pay Scales and Career Advancement Scheme for Librarians and Physical Educators are discussed as a part of

Appendix 1 in pages 80-83. Incentives for Ph. D./M.Phil. and other higher qualifications for these categories in the same Appendix are presented in pages 84-86. Fitment Tables for these categories along with equivalent categories of teachers are displayed in pages 94-98. Minimum Scores for Academic Performance Indicators (APIs) for direct recruitment of teachers in university departments/Colleges, Librarian/ Physical Education cadres is in page 111. APIs for Physical Educators are given in pages 114-121 and the same for Librarians are attached in pages 122-130. This shows that the document discussed specific aspects of Librarians and Physical Educators in just 43 pages, approximately 1/3 of the document.

3. EXPERT COMMITTEE RECOMMENDATIONS

What is the use of an expert committee if its recommendations are not considered by the Government and instead give more weightage to its own bureaucrats? This appears to have happened with the recommendations of the UGC PRC which comprised of eminent educationists and senior bureaucrats. The UGC while preparing the documents [1, 2] for implementation carefully ignored the PRC recommendations in many places. If this is the case, let us have no expert committees and leave everything to Administrators so that they fix everybody's pay and service conditions below theirs. There have been serious grievances on the part of IPS cadre and some defence cadres due to their downgrading compared to equivalent cadres in IAS in the aftermath of the latest pay implementation. No country can progress with efficient administrators only and without excellence in other areas. Two places where the recommendations concerning Deputy Librarians were blatantly violated are:

- Placing only Associate Professors in PB4 and equivalent cadres of Deputy Librarians and Deputy Directors of

Physical Education in PB 3

- Ignoring the recommendations of providing CAS to Deputy Librarians to become Librarians and Deputy Directors of Physical Education to become Directors of Physical Education as in the case of Associate Professors becoming Professors

4. PARITY OF DEPUTY LIBRARIANS

UGC PRC has only put the newly created post of Senior Associate Professor for Colleges in PB 4 maintaining Associate Professor of University/College in PB 3 along with equivalents of Deputy Librarians and Deputy Directors of Physical Education. The UGC Regulations [1, 2] ignoring the recommendations of UGC PRC [3] fixed Associate Professor of University/College in PB 4. While doing so, they have not elevated the equivalent cadres of librarians and physical educators. Thus by keeping them in PB 3, the parity they enjoyed with teachers got broken. Thus UGC should immediately undo the harm done to librarians and physical educators by elevating these posts also to PB 4 like the Associate Professor.

Appendix 1 states there shall be only three designations of Assistant Professors, Associate Professors and Professors in respect of teachers in universities and colleges with no change in the present designation in respect of Library and Physical Education Personnel at various levels [4]. Why is it so? Why can't the Deputy Librarian be redesignated as Associate Librarian and Deputy Director of Physical Education as Associate Director of Physical Education like Associate Professor at PB4 as is being done for renaming the middle level teacher designation of Reader? By elevating the middle level teacher grade to PB4 after keeping the middle level teacher equivalent cadres in library and physical education in PB3, the Regulations attempted to break the parity these cadres have enjoyed for long.

5. PB3 TO PB4 MOVEMENT

Pay scales when changed during Pay Commission recommendations should adopt a new scale considering the present scale. What is being done to middle level teachers and academics is a curious case. The 5th Pay Commission scale for Reader/Deputy Librarian was 12000-420-18300 which is created by merging two government pay scales of 12000-375-16500 and 14300-400-18300. The 6th Pay Commission while revising the scales put the 12000-375-16500 in PB3 and 14300-400-18300 in PB 4. It would have been ideal for the UGC and Government to place middle level positions of teachers and librarians in PB4 instead they put them only at PB3 and suggested that they will move to PB4 after three years in PB3 with AGP 8000. The Government has upgraded Lt. Colonels in Rs 37,400 -67,000 with a grade pay of Rs 8,000 from the earlier announced scale of Rs 15,600 - 39,100 with grade pay of Rs 7,600 [5]. The case of Readers were also taken up strongly by Associations like DUTA and interfaced well with the higher political establishment so that all Readers and equivalent cadres of librarians and physical educators with three years experience in AGP 8000 were placed in PB4 with AGP 9000 without any selection process like interview as per 3.1, 3.2 and 3.3 of Schedule for Clause 6.8.0 [6]. But the Regulations under clause 6.6.5 [7] and 6.3.(iii) of Schedule for Clause 6.8.0 [8] suggest fulfilling other conditions of eligibility as per API scoring system and PBAS methodology laid down by the UGC for CAS promotion for Deputy Librarians to move to PB4 which appears to discriminate between present incumbents and newly appointed. By placing Associate Professors in PB 4, the problem of a Reader to spent 3 years in PB3 will affect only present incumbents and not those who are newly recruited whereas every Deputy Librarian freshly recruited as well has to spent 3 years in PB 3 before moving to PB 4 as per the evaluation criteria proposed.

6. RELAXATION IN NET

Under 3.3.1, the regulations prescribe NET/SLET/SET shall remain the minimum eligibility condition for recruitment and appointment of Assistant Professors in Universities / Colleges / Institutions. Provided however, that candidates, who are or have been awarded a Ph. D. Degree in accordance with the University Grants Commission (Minimum Standards and Procedure for Award of Ph.D. Degree) Regulations, 2009, shall be exempted from the requirement of the minimum eligibility condition of NET/ SLET/SET for recruitment and appointment of Assistant Professor or equivalent positions in Universities / Colleges / Institutions [9]. It remains to be seen whether this relaxation is going to benefit genuine students or those who are 'connected' who have access to everything without good academic record. This may also block the chances of Ph.D. for many of the ordinary students as there is a long queue of students with high connections to avail Ph.D. degree to make themselves exempted from NET for being 'eligible' for future vacancies.

7. CONTRADICTIONS IN THE REGULATIONS

Under 3.7.0, the regulations suggest the Ph.D. Degree shall be a mandatory qualification for the appointment of Professors and for promotion as Professors. In 3.8.0, the Regulations reiterate the Ph.D. Degree shall be a mandatory qualification for all candidates to be appointed as Associate Professor through direct recruitment [10]. No one shall be eligible to be appointed, promoted or designated as Professor, unless he or she possesses a Ph.D. [4]. However these prescriptions were not made applicable to the library cadres (though Ph.D. was insisted for Physical Educators) as per 4.5.0 where the Ph.D. is treated as a desirable qualification only for Professor equivalent cadre of Librarian and Reader (Associate Professor as per 5.1.7 [12]) equivalent cadre of Deputy Librarian [13]. Compare this with 6.3. (ii) of the regulations which prescribe "on completion of service of five years, Assistant Librarian (Sr. Scale) / College Librarian (Sr. Scale) shall be eligible for the post of Deputy Librarian/ equivalent posts in Pay Band of Rs.15,600 - Rs. 39,100, with Academic Grade Pay of Rs.8,000, subject to their fulfilling other conditions of eligibility (such as Ph.D. degree, etc. for Deputy Librarian) [8]. This implies that an Assistant Librarian can become Deputy Librarian without Ph. D through open recruitment whereas it is possible only with Ph. D. through CAS. This again appears to discriminate between professionals working in the same post. May be after convinced of this and to remove the anomaly, the Regulations under 6.3 (iv) suggest that those without Ph.D. can also achieve the grade pays of 8000 and 9000 (preferably with the designation, Assistant Librarian (Selection Grade)/College Librarian (Selection Grade)) [8].

The incumbent teacher must be on the role and active service of the Universities/Colleges on the date of consideration by the Selection Committee for Selection/CAS Promotion [14]. Why is it required for selection is not clear as in open selection candidates from other Institutions can also apply and attend interview.

The experience prescribed for open recruitment to the post of Librarian in the Regulations (see 4.5.1) is at least thirteen years as a Deputy Librarian in a university library [15]. In another portion, the Regulations say "Deputy Librarian completing service of three years in the AGP of Rs.9,000 and otherwise eligible as per the API scoring system and PBAS methodology developed in these Regulations, with a Ph.D. qualification shall also be eligible to be considered for appointment to the post of Librarian through open recruitment" [16]. Since most Deputy Librarians complete service of three years in the AGP of Rs.9,000 in 6 years of assuming the post, it is not clear why the higher experience is prescribed. Is it out of an intention to keep the Librarian post vacant for being managed (?) by teachers or professionals from other streams?

In API points for Category III, the project and consultancy amount for Librarians is kept as per the amount fixed for Engineering/Agriculture/Veterinary Science/ Sciences/Medical Sciences and not as per the same for Languages/Arts/Humanities/Social Sciences/Library/ Physical education/ Management which is more appropriate considering the nature of funding and support for libraries. Otherwise librarians may get lesser points than their counterparts in teaching. Similarly in III (C) (iv), 'Major Policy document of Govt. Bodies at Central and State level' is not added as Librarians are more likely to do this rather than filing patents or engaging in technology transfer. In III (D), the heading 'Research Guidance' is not present. There are no points mentioned for participation and presentation of research papers (oral/poster) in international, national or regional/state level conferences for librarians [17].

The Regulations in the last two lines of last page as a note mentions "For universities for which Sixth PRC Awards (vide Appendix 2) are applicable, Stages 1, 2, 3, 4 and 5 correspond to scales as provided and AGP of Rs. 6000, 7000, 8000, 9000, 10000 and 12000 respectively [18]. The last AGP 12000 is applicable for stage 6 and is erroneously added in this sentence. The word non-vocational is used instead of non-vacational in another portion of the Regulations [19].

8. EXPERIENCE FOR DIRECT RECRUITMENT

An Assistant Professor with eight years experience is eligible to apply for Associate Professor where as teaching experience of ten years (not mentioned whether as Assistant Professor or Associate Professor) is prescribed for the post of Professor. This implies that for a teacher who gets the higher positions through direct recruitment can attain their highest cadre of Professor in 10 years whereas for the cadre of Librarian still the experience prescribed in earlier Pay Commission(s) is copied as it is in the Regulations (see 4.5.1) insisting for at least thirteen years as a Deputy Librarian in a university library or eighteen years' experience as a College Librarian (incidentally a college teacher can become principal of the college with 15 years experience as per the same Regulations) [15]. Thanks to UGC, at least ten years as University Deputy or fifteen years as University Assistant DPEs/College (selection grade) prescribed for the direct recruitment to University Director of Physical Education and Sports post [20]. It appears that either this is a clerical error in the preparation of the document (there are errors in other places also like 'Assistant Professor' is used instead of 'Associate Professor' in the first line of p. 35 or 'universities' instead of 'colleges' in the Note of p. 109 and hence this assumption gets more firm) where earlier experience for the Librarian positions was copied as such without modification or else it is a deliberate attempt to delay and deny promotional avenues for Deputy Librarians. This feeling gets all the more confirmed when one reads "Deputy Librarian completing service of three years in the Academic Grade Pay (AGP) of Rs.9,000 and otherwise eligible as per the API scoring system and Performance Based Appraisal System (PBAS) methodology developed in these Regulations, with a Ph.D. qualification shall also be eligible to be considered for appointment to the post of Librarian through open recruitment" [16]. Even in the earlier 2009 Regulations, experience prescribed for Librarian was "a minimum of 15 years of teaching/librarian experience of which at least 5 years experience as a Deputy Librarian in a University Library or 10 years' experience as Assistant Librarian in the University or as College Librarian" [2].

Ideally it should have been experience of 5 years as University Deputy Librarian and 10 years as University

Assistant Librarian/College Librarian with a minimum total experience of a decade in the profession to apply for direct recruitment to the post of University Librarian like teachers considering the following:

- At the entry level of Assistant Professor/Assistant Librarian, similar qualifications were prescribed. Universities insist for NET/SLET/Ph.D. at the entry level.
- UGC has recognised the cadres of librarians and physical educators equivalent to teachers considering the not so non-significant academic roles they play in grooming tomorrow's citizens side by side with teachers.
- As an equitable democratic society, we practice no discrimination with respect to discipline like caste, creed, religion, gender etc., and that's why a teacher of languages gets the same pay as a teacher of medicine/engineering/science/management. An academic professional position in library must hence entitle for the same service conditions and perks like that of teachers.

Also in the experience prescribed for direct recruitment for the post of Librarian, the mention of University Assistant Librarian is not there though the Regulations equates College Librarian with Assistant Librarian of University. This would help University Assistant Librarians stagnated in their positions to apply for higher position of Librarian. Sometimes elimination of this term may avoid their applications from shortlisting by local administrators. The career progress of teachers and librarians through direct recruitment is highlighted in Fig. 1 and Fig.2 respectively.

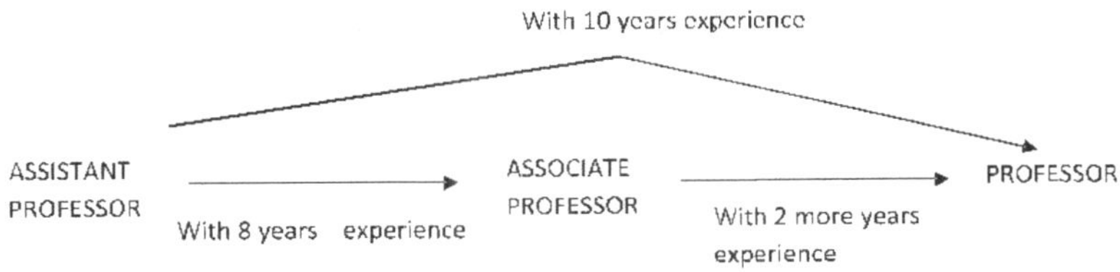

Fig. 1. Career Progression of Teachers through Direct Recruitment

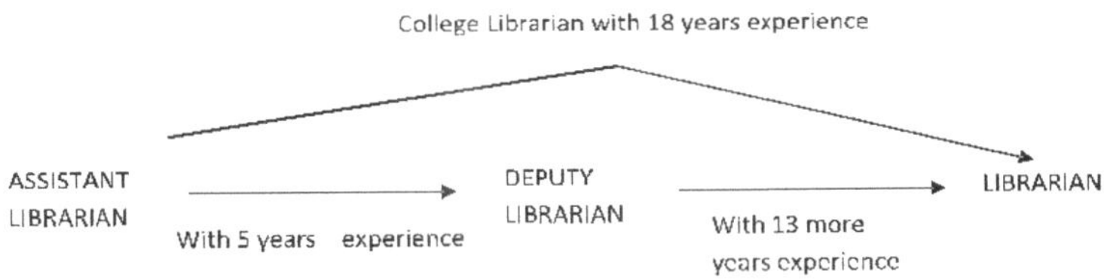

Fig. 2. Career Progression of Librarians through Direct Recruitment

9. SELECTION COMMITTEE FOR PHYSICAL EDUCATION AND LIBRARY FOR DIRECT RECRUITMENT

Selection Committees for the posts of Directors, Deputy Directors, Assistant Directors of Physical Education and Sports, Librarians, Deputy Librarians and Assistant Librarians shall be the same as that of Professor, Associate Professor and Assistant Professor respectively, except that the concerned expert in Physical Education and Sports or Sports Administration or Library, practicing Librarian/ Physical Director, as the case may be, shall be associated with the Selection Committee as one of the subject experts [12].

This indicates that for selecting teachers, all members in Universities and all excepting Chairman in Colleges shall be teachers whereas for selecting librarians or physical educators, selection committee shall at most include one from the stream. The remaining members, to large extent teachers, can tilt the selection process for library sake or for teachers sake can be anybody's guess. At the same time, the

Regulations seem to be extremely concerned about judicious selection of persons for positions like library as evident in the suggestion "in the selection process for posts involving different nature of responsibilities in certain disciplines/ areas, such as Music and Fine Arts, Visual arts and Performing arts, Physical education and Library, greater emphasis may be laid on the nature of deliverables indicated against each of the posts in these Regulations which need to be taken up by the concerned institution while developing API based PBAS proforma for both direct recruitment and CAS promotions" [21].

Ideally the selection process for librarians should involve more librarians and few teachers of library science or other streams (preferably best users of library who have a genuine concern for its well being) all having highest professional integrity to choose the best person to academically administer and efficiently manage an important academic service utility like library. This is especially important as libraries are being influenced by large scale challenges after the advent of information technology and information resources in multiple media, formats and ever increased user demands for better information provision for education and research.

10. SCREENING CUM EVALUATION COMMITTEE FOR CAS PROMOTIONS

The "Screening cum Evaluation Committee" for CAS promotion of Assistant Professors/equivalent cadres in Librarians/Physical Education from one AGP to the other higher AGP shall consist of the Vice Chancellor as the Chairperson of the Selection Committee, the Dean of the concerned Faculty, the Head of the Department / Chairperson of the School and one subject expert in the concerned subject nominated by the Vice Chancellor from the University panel of experts for University positions. In colleges, the Committee consists of the Principal of the college, Head of the concerned department from the college and two subject experts in the concerned subject nominated by the Vice Chancellor from the university panel of experts. Any three members with at least one subject expert/ university nominee form the quorum for these committees in both categories [14]. The Committee for CAS of Librarians should involve more librarians and few teachers of library science or other streams (preferably best users of library who have a genuine concern for its well being) all having highest professional integrity to objectively assess the person concerned without any biases. In some cases, it is quite common that a library professional is rejected/discriminated not for his/her performance but for his/her general conduct such as not yielding to a specific demand by a teacher which is not permissible as per rules or not in the good books of a senior functionary of the university/college.

11. CAS OF TEACHERS

The upward movement of teachers from Stage 1 to Stage 5 through CAS is presented in 6.4.0 to 6.4.9 of the Regulations [22], is presented in Fig. 3. Ten percent of the number of the posts of Associate Professor in an Under Graduate College shall be that of Professors provided that there shall be no more than one post of Professor in each Department with one-fourth (25%) of the posts directly recruited or filled on deputation and the remaining three-fourths (75%) of posts filled by CAS promotion from among eligible Associate Professors of the relevant department of the Under Graduate College and there shall be one post of Professor in each Department of a Post-Graduate College as per 6.5.0 [23]. Ten percent of the positions of Professors in a university, with a minimum of ten years of teaching and research experience as professor either in the pre-revised scale of Professor's pay or the revised scale pay will be eligible for promotion to the higher grade of Professorship (stage 6, AGP 12000), on satisfying the required API score through the PBAS methodology through a duly constituted Expert committee with no interview of candidates, and such teachers shall continue to be designated as 'Professor' [24].

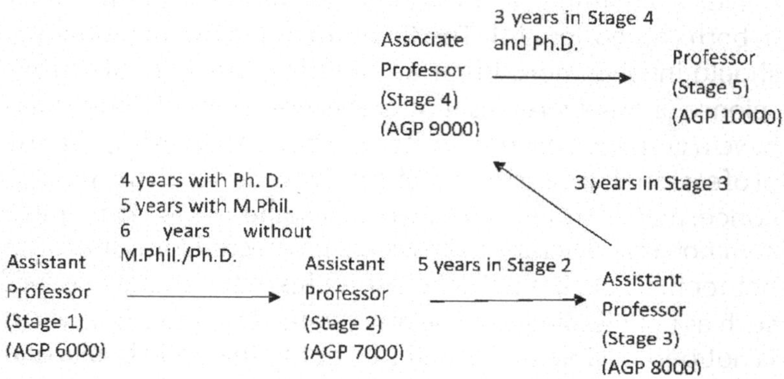

Fig. 3. Career Progression of Teachers through CAS

12. CAS OF LIBRARIANS

Though it is true that an Assistant Librarian like Assistant Professor reaches the grade pay of Rs. 9000 through CAS in 12 years with Ph.D., 13 years with M.Phil., or 14 years without M.Phil./ Ph.D. [25], no avenue is created for a Deputy Librarian to achieve the grade pay of 10000 through CAS, let alone any librarian ever achieving the grade pay of Rs. 12000. May be to fool deputy librarians that they are also getting CAS (reaching PB 4 with AGP 9000 after three years of service at AGP 8000), that Deputy Librarian post is kept at AGP 8000 unlike middle level teacher grade of Associate Professor at AGP 9000 overruling the recommendation of UGC PRC to keep both in the same pay band and AGP. CAS for Deputy Librarian should be the one to reach the scale of Librarian and not anything less than that in the same way as an Associate Professor can become Professor through CAS.

The Regulations exhort that the pay of teachers and equivalent positions in Universities and Colleges shall be fixed according to their designations in two pay bands with different AGPs which shall ensure that teachers and other equivalent cadres covered under this Scheme, subject to other conditions of eligibility being satisfied, have multiple opportunities for upward movement during their career [4]. Perhaps the UGC wants to create different 'multiple opportunities' for teachers and equivalent cadres of librarians and physical educators. The bureaucrats who framed the UGC Regulations ignored the positive recommendation of the UGC PRC that: Deputy Librarians may be considered for promotion to Librarian under CAS on lines similar to and under conditions of eligibility similar to those of Readers seeking promotion to the post of Professor by redesignating the Senior most Librarian as Chief Librarian. College Librarian (Selection Grade) with six years' experience should be eligible for promotion to the post of Senior College Librarian (Selection Grade) under CAS on the same lines as Readers/Lecturers (Selection Grade) are proposed to be considered for promotion to the post of Senior Reader [26]. The career advancement presently offered for librarians by the Regulations is pictorially represented in fig. 4.

13. LIBRARIAN POST ON ROTATION

The CAS currently available to working professionals is too biased and very limited. The CAS is available currently for Asst. Librarians to reach the level of Deputy Librarian only. Here also, relaxations for MPhil/PhD are not granted to Asst. Librarians. So a professional who chose to serve in a library has to retire in the Deputy Librarian level itself as per the current options. Further, to apply for a librarian post, you need at least 13 years as experience as a Deputy Librarian in a University or 18 years experience as a College Librarian.

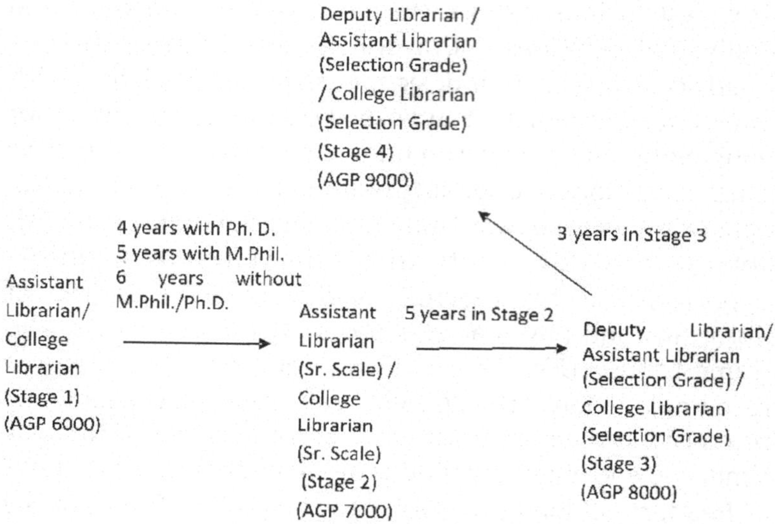

Fig. 4. Career Progression of Librarians through CAS

How many of the Librarians in position in Universities have 13 years prior experience as Deputy Librarian? This implies that there are aliens (who never worked in the University/ Academic stream) by virtue of their previous credentials prowling on the University Librarian position. There are also many Universities keeping the post vacant or being managed it through a Professor cum part-time librarian. This severely impacts the library organisation and information services on the one hand and frustrates the working professionals on the other.

It is evident that equivalent CAS options as available for teachers must be extended to working professionals in Universities, Colleges, academic and research institutions is the rightful due of this category of professionals. Deputy Librarians must be given CAS to become Librarians after 6 years of service in the cadre. One among the Librarians must act as Director (Library)/University Librarian/Chief Librarian (the overall administrative and academic head of the Library) for a specified term of 2/3/5 years as prevalent for rotational headship in other departments of the University. This will also bring in a democratic style of functioning in this august academic service unit in the University. Similarly a College Librarian is extended ample options as available for a college lecturer to move to higher scales.

The biggest hurdle in giving CAS to Deputy Librarians is the fact that post of Librarian is one and it can be given only against vacancy whereas a Professor position is not so, hence any Associate Professor can aspire for that post on CAS. UGC has to really free the position of Librarian in universities and colleges from this 'one post and vacancy based nature' to be a designation for senior library position like Professor for teacher. There was a time a Professor or senior teacher of the Department functioning as Head of the Department till retirement or for long duration. Now all the teaching Departments of a University/College have the Headship on rotation among senior teachers. We have all experienced the benefits of this arrangement as it will lead to more democratic and decentralised decision making, bring in various cultures, influences, abilities in management of the affairs of the Department. Library being a functional academic unit of the University/College also needs this arrangement for further improving its various roles in the education process. There are cases of a good librarian turning not so good due to long periods of being at the top. There are also cases of libraries turning as fiefdoms of the Librarian which is not going to bring in any good for the library or its users/staff. Except a very small minority who is unfortunately greedy for administrative positions, majority of the librarians in position would agree with a rotational headship of the Library from senior professional staff in the library as it will not affect their seniority or perks. The Deputy Librarians should hence can be given CAS to become Librarians and every Librarian should get a chance to Head the Library for a specific duration of three/five years like

Headship of other teaching departments in the University. This is all the more required not just to meet the career advancement of Deputy Librarians but to effectively meet the different challenges of emerging library and information routines and services which call for managing library like an academic unit which needs more academic leadership rather than mere administrative acumen. It is a fact that library has many administrative routines which are very important but its academic responsibilities are more vital.

14. LEAVES

Duty leave of the maximum of 30 days in an academic year may be granted for attending conferences and meetings, delivering lectures, working in another Indian or foreign university, participating in a delegation or working on a committee, etc., which may be combined with earned leave, half pay leave or extraordinary leave [27]. It is not clear whether this provision is extended to librarians as nothing explicit is mentioned in its coverage (only in one place the word teacher is used while discussing about meetings) and can be denied for librarians by local administrators.

Study leave may be granted (two years in the first instance, extendable by one more year, if there is adequate progress) for the entry level appointees as Assistant Professor/Assistant Librarian/ Assistant Director of Physical Education and Sports/College DPE&S after a minimum of three years of continuous service, to pursue a special line of study or research directly related to his/her work in the university or to make a special study of the various aspects of university organization and methods of education. Study leave may be granted not more than twice during one's career subject to the maximum of study leave admissible during the entire service should not exceed five years [28].

Permanent, whole-time teachers of the university and colleges who have completed seven years of service as Reader/Associate Professor or Professor may be granted sabbatical leave to undertake study or research or other academic pursuit solely for the object of increasing their proficiency and usefulness to the university and higher education system. The duration of leave shall not exceed one year at a time and two years in the entire career of a teacher [29]. Only teachers are mentioned as eligible with no mention of librarian cadres.

15. RESEARCH PROMOTION GRANT

The UGC or the respective agency (Central/State Governments) may provide a start-up grant at the level of Rs. 3.0 lakhs in Social Sciences, Humanities and Languages and Rs. 6.0 lakhs in Sciences and Technology to teachers and other non-vacational academic staff to take up research immediately after their appointments [19]. In the case of consultancy projects, the consultancy rules, terms, conditions and the model of revenue sharing between institutions and consultant teachers shall be as per the UGC Consultancy Rules to be provided separately [19].

16. WORKLOAD

The workload of the teachers in full employment should not be less than 40 hours a week for 30 working weeks (180 teaching days) in an academic year. It should be necessary for the teacher to be available for at least 5 hours daily in the University/College. Direct teaching-learning process hours should be 16 hours for Assistant Professor and 14 hours for Associate Professor and Professor. A relaxation of two hours in the workload may, however, be given to Professors who are actively involved in extension activities and administration. A minimum of 6 hours per week may have to be allocated for research activities of a teacher [30].

What about the workload of librarians? The UGC thinks that Librarians like other non teaching and administrative staff will do daily 8 hour chores, sometimes even on odd shifts of night and weekends, and work extra to perform academic research and development activities equivalent to teachers. There should be flexible duty timings and time relaxation in duty hours as for teachers for teacher equivalent cadres of librarians and physical educators too. This would help them to update their skills and improve their knowledge. All work and no rest would leave people dull and this is the reason for the poor work output in many institutions. Why can't even the administration and non teaching staff be provided some extra off days during vacations by maintaining a skeletal staff to do the essential activities? Institution specific duty benefits are permitted in many institutions. This may in turn boost their work output during the normal working period.

17. INCENTIVES FOR PH.D./M.PHIL.

Assistant Librarian/College Librarian or higher positions who have already been awarded Ph.D. in library science at the time of coming into force of these Regulations or having already undergone course-work as well as evaluation, if any, and only Notification in regard to the award of Ph.D. is awaited, shall also be entitled to the award of 3 non-compounded increments even if the university awarding such Ph.D. has not yet been notified by the UGC as having complied with the process prescribed by the Commission. In respect of every other case, the benefit of 3 non-compounded increments (five and two non-compounded advance increments admissible respectively for Ph.D. and M.Phil. to those recruited at entry level) only if the university awarding the Ph.D. has been notified by the UGC to have complied with the process prescribed by the Commission for the award of Ph.D. in respect of either coursework or evaluation or both, as the case may be [11]. Ph.D. is not a one day affair and what about those who are in the midst of the research work. Ideally the Regulation should have excluded all cases where the registration of the candidate for Ph.D. is approved by different Universities with the stipulation having only prospective effect.

Since Deputy Librarians were placed in PB 3, the three advance increments they get on award of Ph.D. shall cease the moment they get PB 4 whereas Associate Professors were able to carry forward the increments. This may also lead to a major difference in emoluments for a Deputy Librarian and Reader/Associate Professor joined on the same day. Considering the movement from PB 3 to PB 4 for Reader/ Deputy Librarian as not a promotion and made due to the genuine compulsions of not fixing these cadres straight away in PB 4, the Ph.D., increments they attained in PB 3 may be permitted to carry forward in PB 4 also. This ensures uniform treatment for those submitting Ph. D. before and after obtaining PB 4.

18. AGE OF SUPERANNUATION

In order to meet the situation arising out of shortage of teachers and the consequent vacant positions therein, the age of superannuation for teachers in Central Educational Institutions has already been enhanced to sixty five years [31]. Subject to availability of vacant positions and fitness, teachers shall also be reemployed on contract appointment beyond the age of sixty five years up to the age of seventy years, be done selectively, for a limited period of 3 years in the first instance and then for another further period of 2 years purely on the basis of merit, experience, area of specialization and peer group review and only against available vacant positions without affecting selection or promotion prospects of eligible teachers [32]. This again creates discrimination between citizens with same qualifications and similar academic experience: if a library science degree holder with UGC NET/Ph.D. joins as an Assistant Professor of Library Science, s/he can serve till 65 years (and sometimes even up to 70 years) and if s/he opts to become an Assistant Librarian, then s/he should retire at 62 (with no possibility of any extension).

Whereas there is no shortage in the categories of Librarians and Directors of Physical Education, the increase in the age of superannuation from the present sixty two years shall not be available to the categories of Librarians and Directors of Physical Education [32]. But the UGC PRC has a different story to tell: one half of the posts of Librarians, 38% posts of Deputy Librarian and 30% posts of Assistant Librarian are lying vacant In universities based on the responses received from the questionnaire survey it conducted [33].

19. PAY FIXATION

Table -3 fits an incumbent Deputy Librarian with basic 12000 in 5th Pay Commission scale to 22320 plus 8000 AGP entailing a revised basic pay of 30320 [34]. There were instances of freshly recruited Deputy Librarians (Associate professors are not affected as they are better positioned in PB4) fixed at basic pay less than this by some institutions. The Regulations suggest a directly recruited Professor shall be fixed at a stage not below Rs. 43000 in the Pay Band of Rs. 37400-67000, with the applicable AGP of Rs. 10000 [35]. A similar mention of minimum basic must have been mentioned for Deputy Librarians as they are not being placed in PB4 like Associate Professors and they share the pay band 3 with Assistant Librarians to take care of such anomalies and counter harassment done by local administrators. Table -5 suggests that a professor incumbent with basic 16400 in the previous scale to 40890 in the new pay band, less than the newly recruits placing at 43000 [35]. Why then that freshly recruited Deputy Librarians should settle for a fixation less

than the present incumbents? It is unclear who is going to sort out these position based discrimination put forth by a national regulator of higher education.

20. PH. D. OPTIONS

Many library professionals right from Assistant Librarian to Librarian used to pursue their Ph.D. on the job by registering with a nearby university on a part time off campus basis. It is a matter of concern whether the new regulations which the UGC is planning to induct for Ph.D. for improving the quality is going to make this degree out of reach for many library professionals. Many institutions have no provision of paid leave for pursuing Ph.D. and many librarians cannot afford to take unpaid leave for this purpose. Nobody can say that all part time Ph.D.s are bad as there are many bad theses emerging from full time research also. A way out to resolve this impasse may be worked out like keeping part time on the job Ph.D. for working librarians, recognising university libraries with qualified professionals for Ph.D. research exclusively for working librarians, etc.

21. API TABLES

The API tables attempt to present different activities related to the concerned positions in three categories out of which only the Category III of Research and Academic Contributions is elucidated with specific points for each type of output. In order to remedy the difficulties of collecting retrospective information and to facilitate the implementation of these regulations from 31-12-2008 in the CAS Promotion, the API based PBAS will be progressively and prospectively rolled out. Accordingly, the PBAS based on the API scores of categories I and II as mentioned in these tables is to be implemented for one year, initially based on the existing systems in universities / colleges for one year only with the minimum annual scores. This annualized API scores can then be compounded progressively as and when the teacher becomes eligible for CAS. For Category III (research and academic contributions), API scores for this category will be applied for the entire assessment period [36]. The Regulations prescribe the following for working out API scores. The Internal Quality Assurance Cell (IQAC) shall be established in all Universities/Colleges as per the UGC/ National Assessment Accreditation Council (NAAC) guidelines with the Vice Chancellor /Principal as Chairperson (respectively for universities/ colleges). The IQAC shall act as the documentation and record-keeping Cell for the institution including assistance in the development of the API criteria based PBAS proforma using the indicative template separately developed by UGC [21]. All universities / colleges will set up verifiable systems for the API related information required in these tables within three months of notification of these regulations. They will have to be documented and collated annually by the IQACs. In order to facilitate this process, all teachers shall submit the duly filled-in Performance Based Appraisal System (PBAS) proforma to the IQAC annually [37]. Whether this decentralised working out of APIs by individual institutions will bring in the desired results is remain to be seen. The Regulations might have attempted to work out scores for categories I and II by eliminating the subjectivity and attempting to quantify the activities so that scores can be optimally worked out by individual institutions as in the case of category III. It is also difficult to quantify many of these activities so that arriving at a rational point system may be next to impossible and hence UGC might have left it to the individual institutions. Some teachers or librarians may be good at recording all what they do in the Institution and present their case well to the evaluators but it is not easy for many to comply.

In API points for Category III, the project and consultancy amount for Librarians is kept as per the amount fixed for Engineering/Agriculture/Veterinary Science/ Sciences/Medical Sciences and not as per the same for Languages/Arts/Humanities/Social Sciences/Library/ Physical education/ Management which is more appropriate considering the funding and support for libraries. Otherwise librarians may get lesser points than their counterparts in teaching. Similarly in III (C) (iv), 'Major Policy document of Govt. Bodies at Central and State level' is not added as Librarians are more likely to do this rather than filing patents and engaging in technology transfer. In III (D), the heading 'Research Guidance' is not present. No points are mentioned for participation and presentation of research papers (oral/ poster) in international, national or regional/state level conferences for librarians [17].

The expert assessment system of 'Selection Committee' is not mentioned for Librarian in Appendix - III Table - VIII (a) [38]. The API Scores in a reduced format as for college teachers shown in Appendix - III Table -II (B), row IV [39] is not attempted for college librarians in Appendix - III Table - V (b), row IV [40] which may lead to confusion in implementation. Ideally these should have been 20/ assessment period instead of 40/ assessment period for College Librarian (Stage 1) to College Librarian (senior scale) (Stage 2); 50/ assessment period instead of 100/assessment period for College Librarian (senior scale) (Stage 2) to College Librarian (Selection Grade) (Stage 3) and 45/ assessment period instead of 90/assessment period for College Librarian (selection Grade) (Stage 3 to Stage 4). In Appendix - III Table -III (C), row I [41], consolidated API score requirement of 300/400 points from category III of APIs appears to be wrong as the maximum score from Category III for the entire assessment period in most cases till stage 5 is less than 150. This may be the total score under the three categories. In Appendix - III Table -IX [42], Orientation and Refresher Course of 3/4 weeks duration is specified for

Librarians whereas the same for only 2/3 weeks is proposed for teachers in Appendix - III Table -III [43]. It is not clear why a librarian should spend more time in a refresher course than teachers.

The Selection Committee criteria/weightages proposed vide Appendix - III Table -VIII (C) [44] indicate librarian positions are more susceptible to subjective assessment than positions of teachers. The weightage of 50% for interview for Assistant Librarian and 30% for Deputy Librarian instead of 20% for both Assistant Professor and Associate Professor is one curious case in point. Why for librarians interview is given more than 20% importance as in the case of teachers is not clear. Academic record and research performance holds 50% weightage for Assistant Professor and Academic background holds 20% importance for both Associate Professor and Professor Positions whereas it is not a parameter for Librarians. Teaching / computer and communication skills by a Lecture demonstration occupy 30% importance for the Assistant Librarian Position which appears to be a far tougher assessment procedure than for the Assistant Professor Position.

22. LIBRARIANS ARE STILL NON-TEACHING

Library staff is treated as academic staff by UGC for quite long. Still there are cases of few universities treating them as administrative or non-teaching staff. There should be a uniform qualifier like academic staff or teacher equivalent staff while library staff is mentioned especially while recruiting and deciding service benefits etc. Extending just AGPs only and clubbing them with administrative staff by disregarding many benefits and facilities of teachers/ academic staff is great injustice. There should be directions to individual institutions about the service conditions and benefits of librarians.

23. TEACHER DESIGNATIONS TO LIBRARIANS

Government of Andhra Pradesh has made a pioneering decision vide G.O.Ms. No. 35 dt. 16-06-2003 to redesignate the University Library Professionals who are drawing UGC scales, i.e. University Librarian, Deputy Librarian, Assistant Librarian and Documentation Officer to that of Professor in Library & Information Science, Associate Professor in Library & Information Science and Assistant Professor in Library & Information Science respectively. If a State Government can take such a pro librarian decision years back, it is high time for MHRD/UGC to implement the same for Central Universities and for other states to follow the same. Maybe to avoid conflicts with teaching departments of Library & Information Science, the redesignated Librarians may be kept as a separate cadre of Library & Information Services (Professor in Library & Information Service, Associate Professor in Library & Information Service and Assistant Professor in Library & Information Service respectively for University Librarian, Deputy Librarian, Assistant Librarian and Documentation Officer) without affecting the seniority or other service benefits of teachers of Library & Information Science. Such a redesignation would no doubt improve the professional freedom of library professionals leading to their better performance resulting in remarkable improvement of library and information services in higher education as comparable with best in other parts of the Globe.

24. CONCLUSION

The higher education scene is witnessing rapid expansion and associated changes and we can meet these challenges only by overhauling the infrastructure, services and evolving new management techniques and functional procedures. Everybody likes libraries and none their librarians is making libraries unable to cope up with what is expected of them significantly. By empowering librarians and giving them their due, none is offering doles or helping them instead the society is indirectly going to reap extra rewards in education, training and research through better library and information services. The Deputy Librarians and College Librarians affected due to negative effects of these Regulations are not able to turn their grievance into reaction due to their small numbers. Had it been the problems of teachers or administrators, it would have got more visibility as a result of the large number of persons in such positions. The library associations and employees unions are doing their bit to voice concern against such injustice towards specific category of professionals. We hope that UGC and others concerned with bringing out these Regulations would suitably amend the proposals for the welfare of all categories of staff in educational institutions so that everyone should perform to the best of their ability to usher in the changes what we are visualising in education, research and development. Perhaps Library Science is the only profession where working professionals are treated so poorly in comparison with teachers in the discipline. Hope that Deputy Librarians would soon get elevation to PB 4, CAS, superannuation benefits equivalent to teachers and all categories of librarians would get teacher designations as done by a very forward looking state of the country.

REFERENCES

1. UGC Regulations on Minimum Qualifications for Appointment of Teachers and other Academic Staff in Universities and Colleges and Measures for the Maintenance of Standards in Higher Education 2010, 130 p., http://www.ugc.ac.in/policy/revised_finalugcregulationfinal10.pdf
2. http://www.ugc.ac.in/notices/UGCregulations2009.pdf, p. 26.
3. http://www.ugc.ac.in/more/5RECOMMENDATIONS OF THE SIXTH PAY REVIEW COMMITTEE. pdf, pp. pp. 64-65.

4. op. cit. 1, p. 76.
5. http://news.outlookindia.com/item.aspx?653202
6. op. cit. 1, pp. 64-65.
7. op. cit. 1, p. 46.
8. op. cit. 1, p. 67.
9. op. cit. 1, p. 4.
10. op. cit. 1, p. 5.
11. op. cit. 1, pp. 72-73.
12. op. cit. 1, p. 36.
13. op. cit. 1, p. 29-30.
14. op. cit. 1, p. 41.
15. op. cit. 1, p. 29.
16. op. cit. 1, p. 68.
17. op. cit. 1, pp. 123-125.
18. op. cit. 1, p. 130.
19. op. cit. 1, p. 57.
20. op. cit. 1, p. 30-31.
21. op. cit. 1, p. 39.
22. op. cit. 1, p. 42-43.
23. cp. cit. 1, p. 44-45.
24. cp. cit. 1, p. 43-44.
25. op. cit. 1, p. 45-46.
26. op. cit. 3, 88-89.
27. op. cit. 1, p. 48-49.
28. op. cit. 1, p. 49-51.
29. op. cit. 1, p. 51-52.
30. op. cit. 1, p. 60.
31. op. cit. 1, p. 87.
32. op. cit. 1, p. 88.
33. http://www.ugc.ac.in/more/3FEEDBACKS FROM UNIVERSITIESAND COLLEGES.pdf, pp. 20-21.
34. op. cit. 1, p. 96.

35. op. cit. 1, p. 78.
36. op. cit. 1, p. 40.
37. op. cit. 1, p. 110.
38. op. cit. 1, p. 126.
39. op. cit. 1, p. 109.
40. op. cit. 1, p. 127.
41. op. cit. 1, p. 111.
42. op. cit. 1, p. 129.
43. op. cit. 1, p. 112.
44. op. cit. 1, p. 128.

Index

F

G

H

I

M

N

O

P

R

S

T

U

V